# what if?

## I Harmed My Children

# Kelly CS Johnson

Published by:
Transformation Books
211 Pauline Drive #513
York, PA 17402
www.TransformationBooks.com

ISBN # 978-0-9968271-4-0
Library of Congress Control No: 2016933074

*Cover Design:* Ranilo Cabo
*Layout and typesetting:* Ranilo Cabo
*Editor:* Allison Saia
*Proofreader:* Michelle Cohen
*Midwife:* Carrie Jareed

Printed in the United States of America

# what if?
## I Harmed My Children

To Nicky, Théa, Ariana and Cole, with all my love always, because that is how we have made it this far and how we will continue to achieve everything we ever wish to.

# Contents

# Disclaimer

The opinions and beliefs that I express in this book are mine alone and they are just that, my opinions and my beliefs. They are not intended to replace or offer any medical advice. But they are also my informed opinions and my informed beliefs. I have done the research, and continue to do so every day, so my opinions and beliefs grow and adapt with my increasing knowledge. Undoubtedly medical interventions save lives every day and there is much to be grateful for. However, they are also acknowledged to be unavoidably unsafe, to have side effects and to cause unavoidable harm to some. Pros and cons, choices: something I never thought about before and something I did not inform myself about, so I did not make informed choices for my or my children's health. I allowed these choices to be made by others, something that I have deeply regretted since as we have had to live with the consequences of those uninformed choices. I now look at both sides, the pros and the cons, of everything and I make informed choices on what I believe to be the best options for me or my children at the current moment. I seek medical advice where needed, then I weigh up the risks and the benefits of this advice and I make my choice for me and my children - for no one else. That is for each individual to do for themselves as is their God given right.

# Chapter 1

What if I harmed my children? What if, without meaning to and with the best intentions, I irrevocably damaged them? I now believe that is what I did. Here is our story.

Decide for yourselves.

# Chapter 2

I married my best friend, Nicky, in 1992. It was me who married him, because left to his own devices, we probably would still not be married and he would never have had any children as he would always have been waiting for the "right time." He's kind of laid back with things like that; anything emotional is a bit of a challenge for him. Give him a piece of machinery to fix, adapt or invent and he's a whiz. If you are old enough to remember the TV series McGyver, that's Nicky, (if you're not, watch an episode and you will see what I mean). For fun we went scuba diving, and as we lived in Ireland where the weather is more often than not wet, windy and cold and you have to hike across muddy fields, rocky shorelines and even abseil cliffs to reach the dive site, that says two things. Firstly, that I was madly in love with him as I am always cold and only started to dive because that was how he spent all his spare time. Secondly, that we were quite hardy and did not give up easily. In fact, I can honestly say that we have never given up when faced with any challenge, though we have often felt like it.

Nicky delights in telling the story about when we managed to sink his much loved first Land Rover Defender, (an incredibly rough and ready vehicle that you either love or hate, for there is always a drip over your accelerator foot when it rains) past the axles up to the underbelly of the vehicle. We were in the wilds of Connemara, miles from anywhere or anyone, and of course it was cold, wet and miserable. We had to dig out in front of and below the wheels and place rocks there, drive forward, dig again and place more rocks behind the wheels and then "rock" the Land Rover out. There was mud spraying everywhere and we were floundering a little when this kind gentleman drove up in his 4x4 which was obviously more used to glamming it around town than roughing it out in the countryside, got out and in an incredibly plummy voice offered his unasked for opinion, "Oh you'll never get out of there without a tractor." He then got back in his car and drove off saying he was on his way to the pub. Nicky says that he owes that guy a drink because from that moment on he knew that we would get out as I would never give him the satisfaction of failing. And we did get out, though by the end, it was hard to tell where the mud in the field ended and we began.

Nine months after we were married, Théa, our eldest daughter, was born at 42 weeks, weighing 10lbs 3ozs. I loved being pregnant and I loved, and still do love, being a Mum. The birth, I was not so keen on. I had a natural delivery but as Théa made her entrance into this world, she got stuck by the shoulders. You could feel the tension in the delivery room; it was palpable. The gynaecologist whipped me onto my side and hooked one shoulder out with his finger and she did the rest. I did everything that I felt was for the best for my child. I breastfed her, I talked and played with her, I took her for all her developmental check-ups and I gave all the vaccinations that our General Practitioner said she should have. When it came to the latter, I quizzed our friend the GP as to the rational of injecting diseases into small babies. He told me of all the graves that he had seen, while travelling when he was young and recently qualified, of all the children who had died of what he termed "preventable" illnesses. Théa thrived and was way ahead of all her developmental milestones, though at the time I was unaware of how unusual this was. She was running around by one year of age and holding full conversations. In fact, later in life one of my closest friends told me that when she would mind Théa she was quite intimidated by her because Théa could hold a conversation with her and having children of her own, she knew how unusual this was. Théa was a serious little child who evaluated and thought about everything. At four she asked me, "If we could stop time, but we could still move, do you think that we could walk on water?" The only illnesses I remember her having were recurrent croup and measles at age one, which I did think was odd as she had recently had her MMR vaccination. However the GP was not concerned and I just looked after her, keeping her in a quiet dark environment and she was fine.

Two years and four months after Théa was born our second daughter, Ariana, arrived. Due to Théa having being so broad shouldered and getting "stuck" on the way out, the gynaecologist induced me at 38 weeks. The decision was mine; he explained that it was my choice but that he felt there was a risk of him breaking the baby's shoulder if he had to hook him or her out which could leave its arm paralyzed if it damaged the nerve, and/or that the baby's shoulders could tear my anal nerves on the way down and leave me incontinent for the rest of my life. Easy decision really, all things considered. He also mentioned in passing that as I was to be induced, the baby would probably be smaller, about 8lbs. I remember going home and crying to Nicky that we would be having a small baby. I had loved that Théa was a beautiful chubby baby right from the start, because her limbs did not seem as fragile as those of the other newborns that I had seen. Ariana arrived quietly into this world weighing 10lbs even. As she was born my gynaecologist looked at me and said, "I may have been wrong about that weight." I was thrilled.

She was a beautiful, easy-going baby who loved everyone. She was as happy sitting watching everyone as she was being held. She was alert to everything and Théa adored her. She would spend hours getting things for her and talking with her, as I did. I did all the same things that I had done for Théa and Ariana, too, thrived. She loved going places and would stay with anyone; everyone loved her. She was an ideal baby with only one frightening and unexplainable bout of projectile vomiting at a couple of months old. This happened every time I fed her for a whole week and each time she could have scored a bull's eye on a darts board from about four feet. I took her to the doctor as soon as it began and he assured me that she was fine and that this was "normal" for some babies. Still it scared the living daylights out of me and I rang the poor man every day saying that nothing had changed and every day he kindly reassured me that all was alright, as she was still having wet nappies and was alert to all going on around her. Ariana also met all her milestones with one exception: she would repeatedly fail the first hearing test every time, but pass it the second or third time round. Again the nurse reassured me that all was fine, some children did this. However, I was concerned, as when she was six months old and sitting on the tiled kitchen floor, I dropped a baking tray behind her making an awful noise, but Ariana never even flinched, just kept right on doing what she was doing. I did tell the doctors and nurses this but again they were unconcerned. "Perhaps she had a cold in her ears at the time?" they suggested. She did not.

While I was pregnant with our third child, things started to change for Ariana and so for all of us. The changes were insidious. We did not really notice them at first, especially as I was also distracted, not so tuned in as I would normally have been. I had a threatened placenta praevia which concerned the gynaecologist so much that he would have me come for a scan every two weeks. When Nicky asked our GP if we would make it to the hospital on time if I started to haemorrhage, he was not sure that we would as the hospital is over an hour from where we live. So each time I went for a scan I was not sure that I would be allowed to come home or whether I would be sent to the hospital straight away. It was like going to trial every two weeks. In the week leading up to the scan I would become nervous that I would be sent straight to hospital and away from my babies (Who would mind them?). Then I would have the scan and the gynaecologist would feel that it was safe for me to return home and I would experience the immense relief of one found not guilty of a crime. The reprieve would last for a week and then it would all begin again. The whole ordeal was made so much worse by the fact that I had no one to accompany me. My parents lived four hours away and were busy with my siblings, some of whom were still of school age. Nicky worked in a family-owned business and felt that it would not be appreciated if he took time off from work unless one of his limbs were falling off or there was a risk of imminent death. I was totally reliant on one lovely friend who had two little girls the same age as ours and who stepped in willingly every time to mind mine.

So it was a while before I realized that it was becoming an ordeal to go anywhere, which was really odd as Théa, Ariana and I loved going out and doing things or visiting people. Now though, Ariana was not so keen when I said that we were going somewhere in the car. Whereas up till now I could just say out of the blue, "Come on, into the car, we are going to...," I now found that if I did that Ariana would say "No," glare at me, suck her thumb and go rigid if I picked her up to put her in the car. Totally different from the child who before would have run to get everyone's shoes for them and ask where we were off to. As she had just turned two, I thought that this must be "the terrible twos" that other parents talked of, something I had not experienced with Théa. I was firm and held my ground. I put her in her car seat and off we would go. As it usually took us half an hour or more to get anywhere, by the time we arrived Ariana would be alright again, so encouraging my belief that she was just behaving badly. However as time went on this behaviour became worse and worse.

Two years and five months after Ariana was born, Cole joined us. Again I was induced at 38 weeks, though this time my gynaecologist refrained from guessing the baby's weight beforehand. Cole, a beautiful baby boy, weighed a healthy 10lbs 4ozs. However once born, he had to be placed in an incubator as his breathing was laboured, due to his forced premature delivery. After a little while he was taken to the PBU (premature baby unit). I was not allowed to go with him and was distraught. The minute they put me in my room, I sent Nicky off to find our baby and told him not to come back until he had. I waited anxiously for what seemed like ages but was probably not even an hour. When Nicky returned, he reassured me that Cole was alright. He said that just as he had arrived in the PBU, a junior house doctor had been about to find a vein in Cole to put an intravenous drip in to give him antibiotics. He had stopped when Nicky arrived and had questioned him as to the necessity of this, as Cole was not sick. Then the doctor's superior had arrived and agreed with Nicky that it was unnecessary. I was not happy; I did not want my baby to be given anything without my consent or knowledge. Nicky reassured me that the senior doctor had said that Cole was just to be given oxygen and observed. He also told me that Cole looked like he was a bit of a "monster" in the PBU as all the other babies were so tiny and some of them could have fitted into the palm of one of his hands. The name "monster" is a nickname that Nicky uses for Cole to this day, though he now fits it better.

I sent Nicky off to get me a wheelchair to take me to the PBU to see my baby as the nurses insisted that I could not walk yet – I would have crawled over hot coals to get there as by then I was so desperate to see him for myself. Nicky found a wheelchair and got me there though the nurses seemed none too happy about me going. But as Nicky explained to them, it would be far worse if I did not go as I would be miserable and so make his, and their lives, unbearable. Arriving at the unit, it was indeed a relief to see our strapping baby and terrifying to see the other tiny little babies struggling with their whole bodies to draw in each breath. The nurses told me that they would feed Cole through a nose tube. I, calmly and quietly, told them that that would not be happening without me having tried to breast feed him first. They were surprised, but humoured me. I took Cole out of the incubator and he immediately latched on and fed beautifully and the nurses said that I could come up and feed him whenever I wanted and that if he was hungry before that they promised they would send for me. They also took a Polaroid picture of him for me to take along. For the four days that Cole was in the PBU, I slept with that picture under my head and the nurses kept their word and were lovely to me every time I came up.

So Cole came home with me from hospital and life went on as before, with me doing exactly as I had done for the girls. Cole, too, was an easy baby. He was happy as long as he was fed and he delighted in being around everyone. He slept in a Moses basket beside our bed at night for ease of feeding. However, shortly after he arrived home, some odd things happened. Ariana began to snore. In the beginning it was tiny little snorts more than snores which made me laugh and I would say to Nicky, "Well, she's definitely your daughter." Then Ariana started to come into our bed in the middle of the night. I just assumed that she felt that the baby was getting more attention than her and let her climb into bed with us. But as the weeks went on, Ariana's snorting definitely became snoring and you could hear her from further and further away.

One night as I was passing the bottom of the stairs, I stopped to listen to her. She was snoring away and just as I was about to go on about my business, she stopped. I thought this odd as her snoring was nothing if not consistent by now. So I climbed the stairs to her room, and by the time I got there she was snoring again. I stood there for about five minutes watching her sleep. She lay on her back with her little fists thrown back above her head looking like the most adorable little blonde cherub you ever did see. I was turning to leave the room again when she suddenly stopped snoring. Horrifyingly, I realized that she was also not breathing, I waited and waited and waited for almost a minute watching to see what was happening. Just as I was about to throw myself upon her and shake her to wake her up, she opened her eyes which then rolled upwards and back into her head, and with a little jump of her body, she started to breathe and snore again and her eyes rolled back and shut! For all the world, it reminded me of a car being jumpstarted. Once I was happy that she was breathing normally again, I flew down the stairs, found Nicky, grabbed him by the arm and started to drag him after me, all the while trying to tell him what I had witnessed upstairs but not able to get the words out fast enough or in anything resembling a coherent manner. So in the end I just said, "Come, NOW!" I am not prone to hysterics, so the wide-eyed distraught stranger in front of him prompted him to follow me at a run without asking questions. Once upstairs, we stood at the foot of Ariana's bed looking at her and I explained what had happened. We waited for what seemed like an eternity but was probably only about 20 minutes to half an hour, and then it happened all over again.

We looked at each other and could see the emotions that we each felt reflected back at us from the other's face. First shock, then fear and then horror that we had laughed about her snoring and missed what was actually happening. How long had this been happening? Was that why she was coming into our bed each night? What if she did not "jumpstart" herself the next time? As it was near enough to midnight by this time, we scooped her up and put her into our bed and along with the baby we all turned in for the night. Neither of us slept at all that night, and the next morning I was on the doctor's doorstep with Ariana and the baby when he opened for business, having dropped Théa to school and looking a little the worse for wear. As our local GP is also a friend, he knows me and knows that I am not one for hysterics or being overly protective. So on that winter morning in the beginning of 1998 when Ariana was not yet three, he listened when I told him what I had witnessed the night before and right there and then made us an appointment to see a paediatric doctor for that afternoon. We all went to that appointment as both Nicky and I wanted to hear what he was going to do for our child and there was no one to leave Théa with and I was still breastfeeding Cole. The paediatrician was a kindly gentleman who listened to what we had to say and then examined Ariana.

After his examination he said, "Ariana's tonsils are extremely large. I cannot see her adenoids but I suspect that they too are very large. When she is sleeping her tonsils and adenoids are falling across and blocking her airway. It is unusual that Ariana does not exhibit any signs at all during the day of this. Normally in these cases the child would be going around with their mouth open in order to breathe. Also, unusually, her tonsils are not infected in anyway. I will schedule an appointment for her to have surgery to remove both her tonsils and adenoids."

I asked, "Is there any chance of them going back down by themselves?"

"No."

"So when will the surgery be?" I fully expected to be sent to the hospital right away as my child was stopping breathing regularly every night.

"Probably two weeks."

"Two weeks?!" I squeaked. And followed it up with, "We have health insurance." For surely two weeks was for those unfortunate enough to be without health insurance.

"I know you do. If you did not you could be waiting up to a year."

Nicky's and my mouth hit the floor and we stared at him as if he was mad. "But she's stopping breathing, several times a night!" I reminded him, because he must surely have forgotten.

"I know, I am sorry. That is as soon as it can be done."

He then went on to tell us that he knew of children who had had to wait on the public health system and by the time they had been given the operation, their chest had deformed in a hollow due to the restricted breathing and that it had never formed properly after that. If he thought that this would be reassuring to me, he was sorely mistaken. I was horrified that in today's so-called civilized, modern world that any child and their parents could be left like this to suffer. How could healthcare and those in it be so callous? Why were doctors not creating an uproar?

"Well, what can I do in the meantime? Aren't there mats that give off an alarm that people put in children's cots when they are concerned about SIDS (Sudden Infant Death Syndrome)? Where can I get one?"

"There are, but they are attached to the child by a clip to their finger or toe, and half the time they come off and so you are running for a false alarm. I do not think that they would be of any benefit."

We left the paediatrician's office dumbfounded and scared. I looked at Nicky and asked if he could believe what we had just been told. He could not. "Well, she will just have to sleep in our bed for the next two weeks and we will have to watch her," I said. He agreed and that is what we did.

When it was time for Ariana's operation, she had to be in the night before. We all went in with her, but as I was feeding Cole and he could not stay in the hospital overnight, Nicky was the one who stayed in with her. The next morning the nurse gave Nicky a small measuring cup with, as he put it, some vile looking liquid in it and asked him to get Ariana to drink it. A few minutes later he gave the nurse back the cup. "Has she drunk it already?" asked the nurse, then, "Quick, where is she?" They both ran to find her. Apparently children were usually slow to drink the medicine and the nurse was afraid, because Ariana was on her own, that when she became drowsy she would fall down and hurt herself. It was fast-acting stuff. Nicky arrived beside Ariana just in time to catch her as she keeled over.

That morning I was on tenterhooks. I hated the thought of Ariana being put under a general anaesthetic. I had heard such awful stories about people not waking up from them and she was so small. I dropped Théa to school and asked my friend to collect her, then I hot footed it to the hospital with Cole. I waited in the corridor outside of the recovery rooms as Nicky was in there with her when I arrived waiting for her to come around. Eventually he came out and said that she was awake. He sounded a little shaken and, when I looked closer at him, his face was definitely ashen under his beard.

"What's wrong?" I asked.

"Nothing, I just got a fright when she came around after the operation. As she was waking up she suddenly vomited up the most enormous blood clot. It was shocking, but the nurse said that it was normal. Well, it wasn't normal for me; it was such a large amount of blood to come out of such a small person. But she's fine now and awake."

Once they moved Ariana back to her room, Nicky went to work and Cole and I stayed with her for the day. That evening Nicky collected Théa after work and brought her in to see us in the hospital. Then, after a little while, Théa, Cole and I went home while Nicky stayed the night again with Ariana. There really was no other way. His parents, for their own reasons, could not and did not offer any help.

Ariana came home from hospital and life moved on.

# Chapter 3

"Does someone up there hate me?" I had to ask myself. As it sure seemed like that to me. After Ariana came out of hospital, we had had several months of normal family life. You know, laughing at things the children did and said, wondering where we were going to get enough money to raise them, pay the bills and finish the house. We adapted to Ariana's changes in temperament by always telling her our plans in advance and avoided changing them if at all possible, and for a time this seemed to work. However, it was still, to my mind, extremely odd that an inquisitive, happy go lucky, easy child should change so suddenly into one who needed structure and hated spontaneity. Whenever I mentioned this to anyone they all said the same, "Oh, I am sure it is just a phase she is going through and she'll grow out of it."

Then out of the blue I started to get attacks of cystitis – if you have been fortunate enough never to have had this let me introduce you to it and also say, "You lucky, lucky sod." The toilet becomes your new best friend and your jailer all at once. You jig up and down, hop from foot to foot and generally look like a child who is holding on too long. You hold off for what seems like forever, but in reality is actually only about twenty minutes since you last went, then you leg it to the bathroom, skidding around the corners, leaping over any obstacles in your way, such as toys, dogs and children, praying that you make it on time and do not wet your knickers. You sit down, but instead of having that immense sense of relief you expect, you grip the toilet seat to stop yourself from leaping right back off again as a pain rips through your nether regions as if you were peeing millions of minute shards of glass. Then before you even get off the blasted bowl, the whole thing starts all over again. I went to the GP's and did my jigging dance in his waiting room, probably much to the amusement of any others present. In the beginning I was mortified and did my best to try to disguise it in, what I thought to be a nonchalant pacing, but in hindsight I am sure I just looked demented. However, as the attacks became more frequent and the drugs stopped working, I couldn't give a damn who saw me, I just wanted it gone. I tried everything, any old wives tale suggested. I drank gallons of water, cut out sugar, ate parsley, which I hate, by the handfuls, and drank bread soda in water which, let me tell you, is beyond nauseating. However, as the attacks increased this odd thing happened, no bacteria was showing up in the tests that the GP ran so he was at a loss as to know why this was happening and also as to what medications to give to help me as we had tried them all. It got to the stage where 24/7 all I could think of was that I needed to pee. If I woke in the middle of the night, and I did several times a night, every night, I would be out of bed in a flash and on my way to the bathroom. Then this constant feeling of needing to pee would prevent me from going back to sleep. It became my constant companion. I could just about make it to take Théa to school before racing back to the bathroom. I did not go anywhere unless absolutely necessary. When all drugs had failed, I was sent for a cystoscopy.

For the uninitiated, a cystoscopy is when they stick a camera up your urethra (the tube from which you pee) and have a good look around your bladder to see what's going on. Thankfully I was knocked out for this procedure. When I came around the urologist came to my bedside and said, "I could find nothing at all wrong. Your bladder is perfectly fine."

"So what do I do now?" I asked somewhat groggily.

"Keep on taking medication."

I woke up double quick. "There is no medication that I have not tried and nothing is working. Nothing is helping with the feeling of needing to pee all the time. Are you telling me that this is my life from now on?"

"Yes", and off he went without any further pleasantries except to hand out a prescription and leave me with the impression that he really thought I was exaggerating everything out of proportion, and maybe even a little mentally unstable.

I looked at Nicky who was looking dumbfounded and burst into tears. I was just 31 years of age, with three young children, and that unfeeling, inhuman creep had been happy to walk off having told me that, as far as he was concerned (and obviously he could not care less), this was to be my life from now on and to get on with it.

This sorry state of affairs went on for over a year. My usual optimism carried me through the first six months but after that I became not a little sad and depressed. The doctor suggested that it was all tied in together and that antidepressants might sort it all out as I had probably been depressed first. So, he too, was now questioning my mental state. Having lost not a little faith in the medical system, I declined. I knew that the cystitis had come first, been around for months and then depression had set in, not the other way around. However, the desperation and depression were very real. Depression, for me, was constantly having a heavy, deep, sad weight in the middle of my chest, making it difficult to continue breathing. Nothing made me smile let alone laugh; it was as if all the joy and love that I had ever known had been ripped from my soul and all the sorrows and pain of the world put in instead.

The only things that kept me going were my children, I did not want them being raised by anyone else. One day while I was driving

Théa to school, with the three children in the car, we had to wait to pull out of our gate as there was an articulated logging lorry coming down the road. I remember the thought flashing into my mind, "If I pulled out in front of that lorry it would all be over." And a split second later it was followed by, "Yes, but if the children did not die with me, who would look after them?" So I didn't, because Nicky would not have been able to look after them by himself. While he loved his children dearly and deeply, he did not know how to show or tell them this. He had no back up and anyway, no one would understand Ariana's needs, I barely did. I began to wonder if there was a God at all, because surely life was not meant to be this hard. If there was a God was he having a laugh?

So out of desperation I went into a health food store and told the poor girl who worked there all about my cystitis and how desperate I was. She had long hair, which looked like it was on its way to being dreadlocks, and facial piercings – everything the medical profession and my upbringing had led me to believe had little to offer in the way of health or sanity. She was kindness itself. She listened to me, gave me some herbs and said, "Have you ever considered homeopathy?"

"No, what's that?"

"It's another type of medicine."

I informed her that I was desperate enough to try anything at all at this stage, even witch doctors. So she gave me the number for a homeopath and I made an appointment.

I arrived at my appointment with the homeopath wondering what on earth I was doing there. I mean to say, my GP and the specialist were not able to help me. They had run out of things to offer except for antidepressants and to tell me to "get on with it" and they had made no contact with me since I had dropped off their radar. So what on earth could this unheard of medicine offer me? The consultation was definitely not what I expected. The homeopath talked with me for an hour or so. She asked me to tell her why I had come, my medical history and my life story. I was amazed. She actually listened to me. Then she blew it. She gave me a couple of little white pills, told me how to take them and told me to come back in a couple of weeks.

I left her office feeling let down again. What on earth could a couple of little white pills do? I had taken a zillion little white, blue, pink and yellow pills in the last year and nothing had worked, so why should these ones be any different? In fact they were probably going to be just like all the rest and I may as well eat a packet of smarties. I mean, really, who had ever heard of homeopathy anyway? Then out of desperation, and because I had nothing left to lose, I took the damn pills. Over the next few weeks the most amazing thing happened, there was the odd hour here and there where I did not think about peeing! The hour here and there increased to several hours together as time went on. I went back for my next appointment with the homeopath and over the next few months the cystitis went away. You have no idea how happy I was not to be best mates with the sodding loo anymore. The timing could not have been better as Ariana was about to start school.

So now, in our story, Cole was almost two, Ariana four and Théa six and I was back to my happy, positive and perpetually optimistic self. Thank goodness. My glass is usually full and occasionally dips, but that is all. I was now completely blown away by homeopathy and decided to do a first aid course so that I could help the children when they got colds, sprained ankles, coughs or earaches and of course, vomiting bugs. Nicky was relieved that I was "back again," as being so uncomfortable with emotions, he had not known how, or been able to, help me when I was sad, because it terrified the living daylights out of him. So his solution had been to spend more time working. He knew that homeopathy had given me back to him and yet could not quite believe that it was a "medicine", so he was sceptical that I would be able to use it with any success in our daily lives. While I was still studying the first aid course, Théa had a severe attack of croup.

This in itself was not unusual; we had steroids in the house as it had happened regularly before. The usual recourse was to create a steam room in the bathroom and give the steroids. We were usually in the bathroom for over an hour and then, if that had not helped, we called the doctor. Oh and of course, it always happened in the middle of the night. This time while Nicky was getting the bathroom ready I gave Théa a homeopathic remedy. Nicky thought that I was wasting my time, though kindly did not say so out loud, but I could read it in the look on his face. However, within five minutes and before the bathroom was ready, Théa's breathing had started to ease and within 15 minutes it was completely back to normal. I slept with her for the rest of the night as we could not quite believe what had happened, but she was perfect and the croup did not return that night.

Ariana was so excited to start school, she had been looking forward to going as she missed her sister and wanted to go with her. For the first month Ariana loved everything about school: her teacher, learning new things, playing with all the other children every day and the routine. Then one month after starting school, I took Ariana and Cole to the GP's for their vaccinations. I had held off on this because I had been wondering if the last vaccination Ariana had received could have in any way been connected with some of her "terrible two" symptoms which, contrary to what everyone had said, she had not "grown out of". Everyone I had questioned, from the GP to my friends and the school teachers, all said that this was absolute rubbish. But I went to the library, (This now makes my children roll around the floor shrieking with laughter, that we actually relied on the library and books to find information as they cannot imagine life without the internet.) where I looked up vaccinations and there were people who were questioning their safety and effectiveness. Only I could not find an unbiased book either way, they were either for or against, nothing balanced and objective. So I felt as if I was damned if I did and damned if I didn't, and even though a small voice in my head was niggling at me with questions like: "No other child you know is acting like Ariana, so how can it be terrible twos?" and

"You know you think this all started shortly after her MMR jab." Its counterpart was going, "Well, maybe they act like her at home and I just do not see it," or "Yes, but my doctor believes in vaccinations. He cares about us and has our best interests at heart and he went to medical school for goodness sake, so he must know that they are safe." I decided to go with what I had been brought up to believe. I cried at night for a whole week before I gave the vaccinations as I did not know what to do. In my gut I felt sick, but who had ever made a judgement on their gut before? What if I did the wrong thing? Also, I was worried about giving Cole a vaccination too as he had had a snotty nose permanently for months now, surely that was not normal. I did not want to inject a disease into him while he already had another one.

# Chapter 4

From the moment Ariana had that vaccination, life went to hell in a handcart. Within one week my child was unrecognisable. All the "terrible two" symptoms escalated out of all proportion. She no longer wanted to go to school or leave me at all. She cried all the time. Our week went like this: Sunday morning Ariana would start to say, "Tomorrow is school isn't it?" By the afternoon it would be, "Tomorrow is school isn't it? I don't want to go." By the evening she was repeating the last question/statement every half hour and crying. We would all try to jolly her along and distract her by doing lots of things that she loved. Sunday night she would go to bed crying and one of us would have to lie with her till she went to sleep. Monday morning arrived and Ariana would wake crying, she would do all that was asked of her: dress, eat breakfast – though a mouse's portion as she was so miserable. But everything took forever because she could not stop crying. Théa would be ready for school and in the car and I would still be trying to get Ariana into it along with Cole. Then when we would get to school, (We were always late because it took so long to cajole Ariana into the car.), Théa would be upset at being late and leap out and I would get Ariana out of the car and take her into school while she desperately tried to stop crying. I would take her to her classroom, where in the beginning her teacher would let her sit at her desk with her, and I would leave. At 2p.m., when

I collected her, Ariana would always be one of the first children out the door and she would be so happy to see me and to be going home. Then after tea, the whole thing would start again.

This went on and got worse over the next couple of months. Soon Ariana was coming into our bed every night and would not sleep on her own, which she had been more than happy to do before. I was not getting any sleep as she kept waking up and "stroking" me for reassurance that she was not alone, so I started to make a bed out of duvets each night on the floor beside me for her to sleep in, (after all, I did not want to molly coddle her, so nothing permanent or too comfortable). Still, in the middle of the night, her little hand would slip under the covers and find mine and I would then sleep with my arm hanging out over the side of the bed, holding her hand, until it froze off or became numb when I would retrieve it back in beside me again. However, within minutes of me taking my arm back into the bed with me and trying to reconnect it, her little hand would be back again, searching for me and reassurance.

Then the teacher decided that Ariana really needed to learn to sit at her own desk, which I could sort of understand, however it only added to the nightmare. Now, every morning on top of everything else, I would have to take Ariana to her desk and, while she would cling to me like a human octopus, I would have to detach her from me limb by limb and place her on one side of her desk while keeping myself on the other so she could not cling to me again. I would then leave with Ariana calling out after me, "Please don't leave me. Don't go." I was an emotional wreck for the rest of the day and each day my heart was broken several times as I did not know what else to do and by law I had to send my child to school, didn't I? Why, all of a sudden, did everything seem to frighten her?

Every afternoon Ariana would tell me exactly what had happened in school that day. She would paint a picture for me; it was as if I was watching a movie with every single detail supplied. Who was there, what they were doing, where they were in the room, what they said, what they wore and so on. She would then ask me why so and so had done or said what they had. It dawned on me, very quickly, that she could no longer interpret people's actions or meanings and was having to ask me to do this for her. I would ask her if they looked happy, sad or cross but she was unable to tell me. I would ask if their voice had sounded happy, sad or cross and she did not know. How could this be? Only a month previously she could tell if someone was happy or cross with her: every four-year-old knows that. But apparently my child did not anymore. She had "lost" this ability. This was what was making school so difficult for her; she could no longer "read" anyone. Naturally, no one could hear me when I told them this. Again I was told that she would "grow out of it," "it was just a phase," and "no, they had never come across this before." When I said that the changes had begun to happen immediately after her vaccination, everyone said, "Really?", in that tone of voice that lets you know that they think that you are, at best, delusional and grasping for straws but really probably barking mad. They also began to infer that I was the cause. "Spoiling her," "letting her away with it" and "if it was my child..." were frequently bandied about with raised eyebrows and knowing looks, within my hearing. When no one believes you, where do you go? Who do you turn to for help? I certainly did not know and no one I asked was offering any help.

This was our life for years. With no help, only hindrance. My family, who would gladly have helped if they could, all lived on the east coast of the country while we were on the west coast, and while they were supportive when we met or were talking on the phone, they could not offer any practical assistance such as babysitting or school pick-ups or even just giving us a break so we could spend time alone or together.

So life went on, weekdays a living hell of misery for Ariana and so by default for the rest of us as well. Théa, who had loved her little sister and been happy to play and be around her, was now extremely short tempered with her and who could blame her? Ariana took up most of my time and everything seemed to centre around her. If Théa and I were talking, Ariana would interrupt because she wanted to understand what Théa was telling me and could not do so without my help in interpreting the context. If we were watching a movie, Ariana would constantly ask questions like, "Why did he say that?" or "What is he doing that for?" thus driving Théa, who just wished to enjoy the movie without a constant dialogue going on beside her, absolutely insane. Weekends were like a reprieve from death row, with all of us being so happy on Friday night (movie night), then waking up happy on Saturday morning and doing things that we all enjoyed. Then Sunday morning the reprieve was rescinded.

Ariana also started to speak very factually and with no empathy. She stated everything as it was, very directly as she saw it and with no filtering.

"Dad, your teeth are very yellow, not white like Mum's." Nicky went straight off to the dentist.

"I always thought that Dad was older than granny (my mum) because he has gray hair and she doesn't and old people always have gray hair." (Ouch!)

These were just statements of fact. She did not see that they might not be appreciated – surely you would like to know if something was wrong so you could fix it. Or that they might cause hurt, in fact she would become extremely upset if she felt she had hurt someone.

As a family, we now find Ariana calling a spade a spade very funny and refreshing, as everything she says is always delivered as a statement of fact, never with any malice. However, not everyone sees it this way and people can become easily offended. In the beginning we did not realise how difficult this would make her life. She has spent much of her life trying to second guess all that she wants to say when she is outside the circle of our family or our closest friends, because she is so afraid that she will cause hurt to someone without meaning to or realising it.

Ariana did have a lovely best friend in school who accepted her just as she was, and outside of school they did get up to a lot of mischief which was so wonderful to see. She was the daughter of my lovely friend who minded the children, and I hers in return, so both families were like second families, Ariana was equally as happy in their home as in ours because she knew that they loved her. Once they both decided to shave, only to come out of the bathroom looking like vampires who had just fed. Another time they made a witch's brew and emptied every tube of shampoo, conditioner, toothpaste and shaving cream into the bath. Then there was the time that their sisters picked blackberries while out on a walk. On returning home, Ariana and her friend danced on the berries, like they had seen people do on the television with grapes to make wine, all over my friend's newly tiled and grouted floor. Funny, innocent moments that made us laugh, however they were short lived and widely spaced out.

Cole started school, the years passed and I was utterly exhausted. Every single school day, Ariana was miserable. At night she would go to sleep in her own bed, more often than not, with one of us holding her while she tried not to cry or think about the coming day. Then, during the night she would wake up and come quietly into our room, to the makeshift duvet bed, where she would lie and hold on to my hand. It affected every aspect of our lives. If we went anywhere, we had to stick to the plan. In fact, if anything, things were getting worse. There were many times that Théa, Cole and I watched in horror as we could see that Ariana was about to have what we termed a "hissy fit." It was as traumatic to witness as to experience. It would happen if we changed the plan, even slightly, or someone tried to force Ariana to do, say, or listen to something that she did not like or agree with. She would go rigid and start to howl, in what I can only describe as a deep, guttural, animal roar. I could not touch her, as she could not allow me. She was obviously in pain but I could not get near enough to help her. After a while her little body would go limp and she would sob and say how sorry she was, over and over. I would gather her up into my arms and she would fall asleep, exhausted. At other times Ariana would start to hit her head off the wall or thump it with her fist and I knew that she was just going to keep going until she hurt herself, so I would wrap myself around her little body like a strait jacket and hold her tight while she fought me to make me let her go. But I would not, indeed could not, she was my baby and she was so obviously hurting somewhere inside of her, so I would hold her until she would go limp and start to sob.

"I am sorry. I don't know why I do this. I can't help myself. You must hate me. You must wish that you never had me. Everyone would be happier if I wasn't here."

While my heart broke, I would reassure her that we all loved her and that we most definitely would not be happier without her. It was very frightening and I had no idea what else to do to help her. I had talked with the doctor and her teachers and anyone else who I thought might be able to help. We ate healthy food, which I made, and limited television to a couple of hours at the weekend. I read to the children all the time, played games with them, took them swimming and for walks. We used our imagination all the time and were forever making tents in the sitting room or going on adventures in the back garden. My life was my children; I adored them and spending time with them. In fact, I know that some people thought of me as "an earth mother" because they told me so. I did not see myself as a hippie, as I no more wanted to camp out for real without a loo and hot running water for my shower each morning than I would have liked to go to the moon! And I liked my bed, which Nicky had made when we moved into the house, it was 6" x 6"6 and I loved it. Why on earth would I want to sleep on the cold, hard earth in preference? But if being an earth mother meant that I was happy to spend all day, every day with my children, playing any game they wanted, talking to fairies and visiting Africa (the back bedroom) to see the lions and giraffes while taking a picnic with us, then that was me. At various stages the rooms in our house have been Africa, the Red Sea, Hogwarts and anywhere else that we wanted to visit but were not able to, due to financial restraints or the lack of being able to find platform 9 ¾! 

So, understand this, I would have done, and still will do, anything at all that I can for my children no matter what age they are. About this time in our lives I realised that if anyone was going to help Ariana it was going to have to be me; that no one else believed me that something was dreadfully wrong and that I was losing her more and more each day. She was slipping away from me; it was as if I was anchoring her in this world, a world which had become a frightening place for her and that she no longer understood without me translating it. I became her interpreter in a foreign land where she did not understand the language or the customs.

By the time Cole was six, Ariana eight and Théa ten I had successfully completed four years of training to become a qualified homeopath. I had seen homeopathy help people and do some wonderful and amazing things. I could give Cole a remedy when he was screaming in pain with an earache and watch, as ten minutes later, he fell back asleep. When Théa had broken her leg quite badly and it had been set in a cast, I had given her remedies to help her body heal itself faster and had seen how amazed the doctor had been that she had healed so quickly and that he was able to remove the full leg cast and replace it with a half leg cast, which he had said was most unusual. I had patients coming to me for homeopathy who were very pleased with the results. I had seen ulcers heal on legs that doctors were worrying would never heal; mothers with postnatal depression bounce back to their joyful happy selves; and children who had suffered with asthma for years stop having attacks. Yet neither I, nor the many eminent and respected homeopaths that I took Ariana to, could help her.

It was not only homeopathy that could not help her. Conventional medicine was failing her abysmally too. After the last vaccination, Ariana kept having repeated burst eardrums. There would be no pain. She would just wake in the morning with pus oozing out of her ear and slip sliding its way down the side of her head creating a sticky, smelly mass in her hair. It smelled vile, putrid! I tried taking her to both the doctor and the homeopath. Several antibiotics and remedies later, the ear would still be oozing and the pus still sliding down her face and the doctor would say that if it did not clear up soon the little bones in her inner ear (the stirrup, the anvil and the hammer

– remember them from your school days?) might well fuse together and make her deaf. Eventually the ear would clear on its own, with me catching the pus on a cotton bud and winding it out of her ear. It was that tenacious and stringy. Oh, and guess what? The doctors did not really believe me that she felt no pain. They felt absolutely positive that it must be sore before it burst due to the pressure. Well, only once did she show any signs of discomfort. I heard her moaning in the middle of the night while still asleep, so I woke her and asked her what was wrong. She said, "Pain," and promptly fell straight back to sleep. I woke her again and asked her where the pain was, "Ear," she replied and again fell straight back to sleep and stopped moaning. I looked at her ear but there was no pus, no redness and when I pressed around the ear she did not flinch or wake. She slept through the rest of that night and in the morning there was the pus but no pain, fever or misery.

Despite what everyone else was saying, "Oh, it'll pass," or "You're spoiling her, be firm and punish her." I heard, on the grapevine, that it was all my fault and I, as a mother, was to blame. I knew that my child was not able to help herself; that she was in pain emotionally and that every day she was slipping further and further away from me and the world she lived in, so I started to do my own research – by now we had a computer at home AND a dial up connection to the internet! (Can you hear the children shrieking with laughter at this? I am positively Neanderthal in their eyes. Dial up connections, where was the WiFi?) Because I had seen Ariana change straight after a vaccination, that was where I started my search. I found that some people thought that autism may be related to vaccinations. Interesting, but not really relevant to us, I thought. Then I learnt that autism was not just the severe cases that I had heard of, where children would or could not make eye contact, could not talk, could not be toilet trained, could not interact with others, and screamed and shouted and flapped their hands. There was a spectrum of autism, like a rainbow, going from the "very severely" affected at one end to the more "mildly" affected at the other end. As you made your way to the "mildly" affected end you had children who could talk, be successfully toilet trained, and keep eye contact, but had huge difficulties interacting socially. The more I read, the more I became convinced that Ariana was on this spectrum. While she seemed to be on the "mild" end, I seriously doubted that the person or persons who had defined it as "mild" had ever lived with a child thus afflicted. There was nothing "mild" about what we were going through.

So again I talked with her teachers, doctors etc, and asked, "What if Ariana's difficulties are autistic traits?"

Again no one would believe me. After all, I was just her mother, what would I know? The inferences were clear: did I have a degree in teaching, medicine or psychology? No? Then, back off and leave it to the professionals. We are the ones who know best. You are just some overreacting, spoiling, useless parent.

# Chapter 5

So we slogged on. It was as if life had become one big quagmire – so much nicer sounding, don't you think, than bog, swamp or marsh? We were on one side floundering and seemingly alone in the rain while everyone else was on the other side living in the sun. Every day we desperately jumped from one dry hillock to another trying to make it across without misstepping and sinking down into oblivion and desperation in the black, sticky, glutinous bog in between. Whenever we met someone along the way, who we thought could help us, we would ask for help, but they would either look straight through us, or try not to see us because we made them feel uncomfortable, or they would just shrug their shoulders and walk on by.

The harder things got, the longer hours Nicky worked; it was just his way of coping. His upbringing had not equipped him to deal with or express emotions, so the rollercoaster we were experiencing at home was just out of his league. I myself was barely hanging in there. Over the years this has truly been the one major bone of contention between Nicky and I. I resented that he worked such long hours and could not help me either emotionally or physically, that effectively I raised the children on my own, with the help of friends when I was desperate. His answer was that he was earning the money to allow me to do so, which was true. But his salary certainly never reflected the hours or effort that he put in, nor did it compensate for the fact that I was effectively a single parent and that I missed him, my best friend, desperately. He was also bewildered and hurting and had no support.

Because school life was so hard for us, I would try and make the rest of life one big party if I could, to distract us and make us happy. The children would have friends over and they would make up wonderful games. The general rule was that as long as no one or thing was in danger, and everyone was being nice to each other and including anyone who wanted to play, anything went. They would raid the kitchen and blanket chest and build Indian villages in the back garden, living a whole lifetime in one afternoon. When it came to bedtime they would frequently have to go and retrieve the duvets they had abandoned somewhere along the way, and they would invariably need a bath! We went to see any Disney movie that came out. As often as we could we lost ourselves in a wonderful world restricted only by our imaginations, which were boundless! We would spend the early part of the summer holidays in the wilds of Connemara, right beside the sea, in a small cottage that Nicky's parents owned, each child bringing friends with them. I would take the children out of school early, as would a friend of mine whose family had a cottage across the bay and who had grown up with Nicky and had children of similar ages to ours. The cottage would be lent to us for two weeks during the summer months and, as no one ever used it during the school term, Nicky would ask his parents for the first two weeks so that we could extend our time there by pulling the children from school early. We would live the life that is described by Enid Blyton in the *Famous Five* or *Secret Seven* books: absolutely idyllic! The cottage itself was a single storey white-washed stone building with a main living/kitchen area with one bedroom off each end. At one end, one of the bedrooms had been cropped to give a small bunk room through which you had to walk to get to the main bedroom. There was no electricity, only gas and all the hot water came from a back boiler behind the fire so this was kept going all day, every day. At the front of the house, a porch had been added and a tiny bathroom put in. We loved it and our escape from what had become our day to day reality. I say "we," as if we all went for the full time, however, this would not be quite the truth. Nicky would come and go, as his work allowed, and we would adore and cherish any time that he was able to spend with us, while appreciating every moment that we, the children and I, spent there.

# Chapter 6

When Ariana was nine years of age there were some changes in the local school which were to affect her, and us, deeply. In the end we benefited from them, but there was a lot of pain along the way. The school was a small village school with three teachers. Suddenly the principal and one of the other teachers decided to retire early. They were both lovely and had helped us in many ways over the years. The new principal was young and arrived at the school with lots of energy and gung ho enthusiasm. Shortly after his arrival, I had a meeting with him where I explained that Ariana had many fears when away from me. I told him in detail of how she reacted to change, the many situations that arose during a normal school day which could provoke such a reaction, and that I thought these could be autistic traits. The meeting lasted about half an hour, me on one side of the table, him on the other, and as I talked I could see his face changing from one of interest, to one of knowing and I knew that he had stopped "hearing" me. He said nothing at all while I talked, did not ask any questions and when I finished my monologue he stood up, shook my hand and said how nice it had been to meet me. My heart sank to my boots and with a heavy step, and heart, I left.

My fears were soon realised. Mr D began to make changes. He would not tell the children about them beforehand, just announce that from now on this or that would be what would be happening. Ariana became more and more upset, so we arrived later and later to school. In fact, we arrived only a little late to the school car park and Cole would head on in, but it could take me half an hour or more to talk Ariana into entering the building. Thankfully Théa was now in boarding school and so spared this drama. I again tried to talk to Mr D, but the realisation suddenly dawned on me that he had missed being born in the correct era by over 100 years, his approach being so Dickensian! He was determined to make "his" school the best in the area. He was convinced that he knew what was best for all the children and, of course, they could all fit in his "one size fits all" approach. There would be no need to make any special allowances. I went home and cried again from sheer frustration and weariness. Why could no one but me see how much Ariana was struggling? Why did everyone insist that it was my fault that I was making her like this? I had two other children who had no difficulties leaving my side; in fact they were often happier off exploring life by themselves and I was raising them all in exactly the same way.

One day when we arrived at the school, Ariana was crying as usual and asking, "Please take me home today. I will be so good, I will not annoy you. I will clean the house, anything you ask me to do, just please take me home with you Mummy, don't leave me." Every single day my heart, and hers, were ripped and shredded, but this day was to be worse. After I had managed to get out of the car and to take a step towards the school, telling her that she would have fun and like it once she was there with her friends, she flung herself back to the car, gripped onto the door handle and said in the saddest and most desperately forlorn voice, "I wish that I had a knife and that I could stab it into my heart so that all the blood would run out because then I would never have to go here again." I gathered her up and put her back in the car and went home. Nicky talked with our doctor, a very kind and calm friend, who suggested that we take Ariana out of school for two weeks and see how things went. So we did and Ariana was immediately happier. Cole had to go to school on his own, but because he is such a laid back, loving individual, he was not jealous. Now here is an odd thing, Cole was going to school without making a song and dance of it while his sister was at home with me having fun, and still my detractors were adamant that I was to blame for Ariana's fear of leaving me. Poor Nicky got the worst of it, as by this stage I only talked with those that were kind to me and I never went anywhere that I felt I would have to talk with someone who disagreed with my parenting. If I was unfortunate enough to bump into anyone, I simply left at the earliest opportunity. Nicky, on the other hand, could not avoid meeting his family and others through work and was subjected to unsolicited views and opinions, many of which were neither kind nor helpful and certainly did nothing to bolster our already strained marriage.

Eventually, Mr D broke.

Looking back, I think it probably had a lot to do with the fact that he, nor either of the other two teachers in the school, had any children of their own. It is a rare person without children who can empathize with parents and understand the pain and powerlessness that they feel when they are watching their children suffer and do not know how to help them; the fear that can grip your stomach in the dead of night when your child is screaming with pain, has a high fever and you really cannot decide if their neck seems stiff and sore when they move it; or the endless days of misery for your child who is visibly withdrawing from a world that no longer makes any sense to them. When I try to describe the latter to people, I tell them it was as if Ariana was slipping away, retreating inside of herself to live in a world of her own, and one that did not cause her pain. Then there was the very real fact that while she was in this world, a lot of the time she felt that she would rather be dead than suffer any more pain. She meant this as a fact; there was no melodramatics or hysterics, just a statement that she did not know if she could go on much longer like this. It was as if I was the only thing anchoring her here, that I was holding on to her with all my might and still we were being steadily dragged towards an abyss. There were furrows in the ground behind me where my heels had ploughed through the ground.

Anyway, back to Mr D breaking. One day, after eventually persuading Ariana to go into her classroom, Mr D stormed out and started to yell at me that this just simply wasn't good enough, I was disrupting all the other children and that it was not fair on them that they had to arrive on time and Ariana did not! I asked him what he suggested as we were doing the best we could. He had no suggestions other than to shout more about how unacceptable it was. By this time, I was backing away from him and had both my hands up in front of me, palms up in a "stop" position, as he yelled and advanced towards me. Eventually, his tirade ceased long enough for me to say that I would meet him after school ended to discuss things. Then I turned and fled out the door to the car, bursting into tears on the way, feeling sick that I had left the children in the school, a place where there was obviously such animosity towards us.

I called Nicky from the car and at first was so incoherent that he could make no sense of what I was saying. When he did, he was all for coming down to the school right there and then and having a go at Mr D. Part of me would really have liked to let him, but the rational part of my brain knew that this would only have made the children's lives worse. So after a while, I limped home. I could do nothing for the rest of the day except call my wonderful friend and ask her to take the children after school while we went to our meeting. By the time we arrived for the meeting, I could not speak to Mr D. He, on the other hand, seemed to have had plenty of time to reflect on his earlier behaviour and was keen to offer his apologies, which he did, several times. I truly could no longer talk to him. It just was not physically possible; my throat seized up at the very thought, so I just followed Nicky into the room.

I do not know what we expected, but it certainly was not Mr D's opening gambit. After we sat down opposite him he lent into us and said, "I have only ever seen one case like Ariana's before and that was an abuse case."

Nicky and I both looked at him completely stunned! Was he seriously saying that we were abusing Ariana? He knew nothing of our home life, had never been to our house, nor asked how Ariana behaved at home. In fact, until a few weeks previously, he had not even known that Ariana and Cole had an older sister because he simply did not care enough about each individual child to find out about their life. I went ice cold with fear as I thought how easy it would be for him to make this allegation to social services and rip our lives asunder.

Nicky lent in towards him and said in a quiet, controlled, ice cold voice, "Be very careful what you say next, because you are now threatening my family."

Mr D immediately sat as far back in his chair as possible and said, "Of course I am not suggesting that that is what is happening here." But of course, that is exactly what he was saying. Why else say it?

The meeting went nowhere after that; just around in the same circles as over the last six or so years. Ariana did not play at break times with her peers, instead she would chat with the younger children. Apparently this was a problem for Mr D, but as Nicky pointed out, she was happy chatting with the younger children and was not off by herself in a corner; and she regularly had friends over after school to play, so we did not see any problem there. Of course, there was her upset at coming to school, but when asked, Mr D again had no suggestions on how to overcome this. I left that meeting more terrified than I had ever been before in my life. Would social services turn up on my doorstep to take Ariana away from us?

# Chapter 7

By now, most people would think that we, as a family, had more than our fair share of fun in life, I know I certainly did; but apparently God thought differently. Right about here in our story I decided that there wasn't a God, or if there was, he was one hell of a vindictive sod, because what happened next really and truly almost broke us completely. This is my diary entry for March 26th 2006, when Cole was just eight years old.

*My darling Cole, My heart has been ripped out of my chest, torn in half and yet I am still breathing, still living. I do not know how that can be possible. We are in hospital, you and I, and the doctors have just told us that you have type 1 diabetes. You are looking at me and waiting for me to tell you what that means, but I do not know if I can even speak anymore! Thoughts are flying through my head, and yet, everything seems to be moving in slow motion. I feel like I have just been wiped off the face of the earth by some malevolent storm. I am floating in space, held on to reality by a few brittle threads that could break at any moment; and yet I must get back because you need me. Please God, let the threads hold, let me be able to get us through this.*

*I hold you tight and start to explain, as best I can, and all the time all I want to do is cry.*

*"You know how you have been drinking a lot of water recently? You know, it seems that you can never get enough? And I have been joking with you that you must be turning into a camel, or that there is going to be a water shortage – which of course would be totally ludicrous as we live in the land of the rain. Well, what has been happening is that your body has been getting sick. Normally in your body when you eat food, it is turned into sugar and floats around in your blood, then it gets from your blood into the rest of your body using a special liquid called insulin. The insulin works like lots of little keys. If your body has no keys the sugar stays in your blood, which is not good because the rest of your body starts to starve because it has no food, while your blood starts to turn into golden syrup - sticky and not able to move around your body very fast anymore - and all this makes you feel sick, and you get very thirsty because your body wants you to drink more so you can pee the sugar out of your body. Well, for some reason your body has stopped making the keys. So now that we know what is happening we can give you some keys/insulin."*

*I know that it will be an injection, but how do I tell you that? God, please let it be me instead of my baby, he is only eight years old! How do I watch him suffering, knowing that I cannot make it better? I am his mother, I have always been able to make it better, or his father has always been able to mend "it", if "it" has broken. Now we are going to let him down, how will he survive our failure? How will we?*

*You tell me that that is ok then, where is this insulin/key stuff? Give it to you now so that we can get out of here and get on with the fun of our lives. What are we waiting for? Come on Mum, let's go! This has always been your attitude to life. From the moment you were born, you have not stopped going. It is as if you are some type of spring. You leap out of bed in the morning – usually at the unearthly hour of 05:30 or 06:00, and rush headlong to meet the new day, with endless fascination and joy at the promise of all that it can possibly hold; and then you fall into bed at night, still protesting that you are not in the slightest bit tired and that there is so much more that you need to do before you can possibly go to sleep. Yet the moment your head touches the pillow, it is as if the spring has finally uncoiled fully, and you fall asleep instantly. And now I have to tell you something that is going to encroach on your carefree, devil-may-care attitude. How do I do that? I do not want to rein you in; I do not want to allow anyone, or anything, to change your zest for life. I feel something stirring within me, what is it? More sadness? No, I think that it is anger.*

*I take a deep breath.*

*"Cole, the insulin is not a medicine on a spoon. Unfortunately, it does not work if you take it like that because your stomach eats it up before it can get into your blood. You have to have an injection, lovey."*

*I watch as your face blanches with horror and then your mouth drops open in disbelief. I can see the defiance setting in as your body stiffens and your eyes glisten and I know, before you even open your mouth, what you will say.*

*"No way! I'm not having an injection! You can't make me!"*

*Dear God, this is so unfair. This stinks. For that is exactly what I must do, I must make you and you do not even realise the worst of it yet.*

*"Sweetheart, the only way the insulin will work is if it is taken by an injection, and it is the only thing that will help you get better. I am so sorry, I wish that I could make it be some other way but I can't."*

*"Why can't you just give me a remedy? You can every other time I get sick and they always make me better."*

*Here is the first time in your life that you will realise my fallibility, that I am human and cannot fix everything. It is so hard and it should not be so. Not at eight years of age. I should be able to protect you, and I cannot. I am a qualified homeopath and between us, our local doctor and myself, we have always been able to make things better for you when you have been sick. Now we cannot.*

*"Cole, I will give you remedies to help you, but we cannot wait. You need insulin now or you will just get sicker and sicker."*

*I will, I promise you, give you remedies to try to stimulate your pancreas into producing insulin again, and I will never give up trying, I promise, on my life, I promise.*

"Mum, I'm scared of injections. It'll hurt, but I'll do it because then we can go home."

*Here is the crux of the matter, the bit I have been dreading telling you because I know that it will devastate you.*

"That is very brave of you lovey, but there is one other thing. You see Cole, because your body is not making its own insulin, you are going to have to give it the insulin it needs every day." *As I am speaking, I see the truth dawning on you and the terror that is spreading, not only across your face, but through every part of your beautiful little body.* "The doctor says that you will need to give yourself two injections every day." *I want to cry out, my insides are being wrenched apart. What must it be like for you? I want to pick you up in my arms and run as fast as I can away from this horror, I want to keep running until it is so far away from us that it cannot get us, but I can't, I cannot save you from this, I am so, so sorry, I am failing you.*

*I hold you and we both cry. We cry because we are afraid, because life as you have known it, and I have known it through you, has ended. It is as if your life has died, not you but all that you knew and that we took for granted. I cry also because I know that it will only get harder for you; that what you do not realise yet is that everything has changed. You will no longer be able to eat what you want, when you want; skip meals if you're not hungry; fast without worrying when you are sick. You will not be able to be the carefree little boy that you have been; never again will you be able to launch into some raucous and wildly active game with abandonment and without thinking. From now on it will be a constant game of balancing: balancing the amount of insulin that you give yourself with the amount of food that you eat and the amount of exercise that you do. It is a game that neither of us wants to play, and yet we are being forced to, because if we do not you will die.*

*The nurse comes in with what looks like a large, old fashioned fountain pen. She shows it to us and explains that this is the injection. You literally claw your way over me to get away from it, so I ask her to wait a minute. I manage to turn around on the bed, on which we are sitting, with difficulty, as you are now using me as a shield between you and the injection. I must pry your fingers loose from my back where I am sure that they would have fused with my skin if that was at all possible. You cling to me and I talk to you; but I cannot offer you the reassurances that you are looking for. I cannot say, "It will be alright," because it so obviously will not. I cannot say, "It will be over soon," because it will not, this is it, for the rest of your life. So instead I tell you, "I will be here with you Cole, I will stay with you and we will get through this; you will be able to do this."*

*"No, Mum, I can't! I can't stick a needle into myself. I can't do it Mum. Please don't make me. Take me home. PLEASE!"*

*I hold you too me, just as fiercely as you cling on to me, and I cannot speak for the moment. All I can do is feel your terror. It is palpable. It is all around us, we are suffocating in it and I cannot rescue you. I cannot save you.*

*The nurse comes to our aid and says quietly, "Cole, why don't you just look at the pen and I can show you how it works and you can see that the needle is really very small."*

*You bury your head into my chest and shake it vigorously. I take a deep breath and say gently to you, "Cole, you have to do this. I will help you."*

*"What if I don't do it? What will happen to me?"*

*"You will get sicker and sicker. You would feel really horrible."*

*"And if I still did not take it?"*

*I can hardly say it. "You will die." You are so white that you might already be dead; but you are not, and I am not going to let that happen. I will not let you leave me!*

*"I don't want to die."*

*"I know that lovey, and I am not going to let that happen. Come on, let's just look at the injection and find out how it works."*
*I turn us around in the bed and we listen to the nurse as she explains how the injection works. It is really quite an ingenious gadget, and at any other time I would be very impressed with its cleverness. It has a cartridge in it that holds the insulin, where a pen would have the ink. You dial up the required amount of units of insulin by just twisting the end of it. The needle, which is where the nib would be on a pen, is indeed quite fine and not too long, about the length of the pink bit of my finger nail, but still indisputably a needle. Once the needle is in the body you press the dialling end back into the pen, like a plunger, and the insulin is injected into the body. You inject yourself in the upper leg, the tummy, the bottom or the upper arm. But today I am not impressed; today I just hate it.*
*You, and I, are both visibly shaking at this stage. You look at me and say, "I just can't do it Mum, I can't," in the quietest little voice that I have ever heard you use in your whole life.*
*"I can do it for you for the moment," says the nurse; and we both look at her as if she has six heads and has gone totally mad. You, I suspect, because you cannot believe that she would be daft enough to think that you are going to allow her to get anywhere near you with that thing! And I? Well, I cannot imagine allowing anybody else to inflict pain on you, and because I know that I have no choice. I have to do it. That we will not be leaving this hospital before either you or I, and realistically I know that it has to be me, are able to give you the injections.*
*"Cole, I will do it for you," I say; and I feel as if I am watching this scene from somewhere far above, that I am floating outside of my body, that it is not really me saying these things, and yet it is. I ask the nurse how you put the needle in and where exactly.*

"I can't watch, Mum."

"That's ok. Just sit on my knee and turn your head around into my shoulder."

"Don't tell me when you are going to do it."

"Ok. I won't."

So you sit on my knee, with a leg straddled either side of my waist, bury your face into my shoulder, put your arm around my neck and hold me in a half nelson that any wrestler would be proud of. In complete terror, I stab the needle into your beautiful little thigh and you, naturally enough, flinch and start to cry. I manage to depress the plunger, and remember to count to 10 after I have put all the insulin into you and before I pull the needle back out. By now tears are running down my face and I cannot speak. I cannot say anything to reassure you or console you; I cannot speak. I take the injection out and give it back to the nurse, dropping it into her hand as if it has just scalded me. She is great, she realises that I cannot speak and that I do not want you to know that I am crying. She talks to you, not silly talk as if you do not understand the severity of the situation, but proper conversation.

"You were great, Cole. You did really well."

"I was scared and it hurt."

"Yes, it does hurt but you were very brave letting your Mummy do the injection."

I manage to stop crying, and she puts her hand on my shoulder and asks if I am alright. I want to yell at her that, no, I am not alright, I am far from alright! That I think that I will never be alright again. But instead I just nod and let her leave the room, for I know that it is not her fault. She has been lovely and extremely caring, just as all the *other members of the medical staff that we have come in contact with here have been.*

*We get changed for bed and curl up in the same narrow little single child's cot, even though there are two of them in the room. We put up the cot sides to stop either of us falling out and look and feel like sardines squished into a can, but neither of us cares, neither of us wants to let the other go: we are afraid that the other will not be there when we wake up. It is late, well past midnight, but it takes us a while to go to sleep, and when we do, it is a sleep so disturbed and haunted that it can hardly be called sleep.*

When we ended up in hospital, we were told that we were among the "lucky" ones. Imagine that, we were "lucky", yippidy do da day, praise the Lord, roll out the barrels and let's celebrate. We sure did not feel lucky, but the nurses assured us that this was true. The reason for this being, that as most people know little to nothing about type 1 diabetes, parents are unable to recognise the symptoms, the massive increase in thirst, the bedwetting that therefore accompanies this, the general malaise or feeling of being unwell, and so the child lapses into a coma before they realise that something is massively wrong. Because I was in a health profession, I had been suspicious when Cole had suddenly started to go from drinking three to four glasses of liquids a day, to running in from outside and throwing himself under the tap and drinking pints upon pints of water. Then he started to have accidents at night, a thing that he had not done since he was potty trained at two. So, after a week of this, I naturally had the doctors test his urine for infection. It came back negative. During the following week things continued as the previous week, only now Cole seemed to be tired and complained of having a headache now and again. So I had to face what I had not wanted to the week before: the nagging suspicion that this could be diabetes. I asked the practise nurse to do a blood test for it. She was more surprised than I was with the results, but her world did not fall apart and mine did. It disintegrated right before my eyes, with me madly trying to hold all the pieces together in my hands even as I watched them slipping through my fingers, like water through a sieve.

Life stopped. I forgot how to function normally anymore. I even felt as if I had to remind my body to breathe at times. Everything that I had done automatically before, flew out the window. My sole thoughts were how to survive and how to keep Cole alive. In the hospital I actually forgot to call Théa, who was by now in boarding school, to tell her this devastating news. I forgot about my beautiful first born child, something that I would never have been capable of before. When, the previous summer, Théa had decided that she wished to go to boarding school as her father had done, I had found it a gut-wrenching experience. I truly felt that I would have coped with losing a limb easier than I did allowing her to go to boarding school. For days after she had gone, I would find tears coursing down my cheeks at the oddest of times; and each time she returned to school after a weekend home I would miss her dreadfully, and yet here I was forgetting about her and her feelings. Ariana, however, remembered her and called her on the first day we were in hospital so that she would not feel left out. Théa was deeply wounded by this error on on my part, and at 13 just could not understand how I, or her father, could not have been the ones to call. This wound and sense of abandonment has lasted for many, many years, and while she now understands that we did not mean to hurt her and has forgiven us, I know that sometimes she still feels the pain of that young child.

I did call three people. My father, not my mother, because while I wished to call her, I knew that if she cried I would completely fall apart, and I could not afford to do that. My hold on reality was so tenuous that it could not afford to be shaken anymore. So I called my father, whom I have never seen cry in my whole life, and told him. His reaction, and that of my mother when he told her, was what I expected. They dropped everything and immediately came to my aid. I also called two friends whom I knew would just be there for me, would not offer any ridiculous platitudes, would not try to "make things right" when they could not, but who would just be there, present, silent and listening, doing whatever I wished. They, too, came immediately. I will never be able to thank any of them enough for responding in the way that I expected and for not letting me down; nor, I suspect, will they ever truly be able to understand how much this meant to me.

Nicky and Ariana came into the hospital every day and we "camped" out in Cole's room, learning the basics of what we would need to know to keep Cole alive. It was surreal. The alien smell of the hospital soaked into every pore of our bodies so that we all started to smell the same as each other, and everyone else in the hospital, so losing our uniqueness and individuality. While the medical staff were lovely, it was easy to see how people – both patients and staff alike – can become institutionalised. In order to deal with, or help, the growing number of people becoming sick, the current medical model has adapted a "one size fits all solution" for each disease. That is, they assume that what works for one person in a particular disease or illness, will also work for every other person with that disease. They no longer have the time, the ability or indeed the latitude, to deal with each person as an individual. People are grouped together by their disease and defined by that disease. The fact that they all may live very different lifestyles or come from different backgrounds, no longer can be taken into consideration. One's individuality is chipped away at very quickly and life can easily become very grey; though, for the time we were in hospital, ours remained very much the black of your worst nightmare, where we were locked in a dark world unable to see a way out because there was no light at all, just feeling constant terror. We all hated it and desperately wanted to leave. One of the friends who I called, and who is also Cole's godmother, arrived bringing with her the biggest remote control car that we had ever seen! It brought colour and hope into Cole's black and terrifying world. She also brought her son, whom Cole idolised, who was several years older than him and so, in Cole's eyes, so very cool. My other friend came too with her son, my godchild and one of Cole's best friends, again bringing light and love.

These were the only times in the five days that we were in hospital that I glimpsed a glimmer of the child I had known.

The wild, tearaway, devil-may-care child I had had was gone, replaced by a changeling who looked like him but who had become my shadow, constantly by my side. If I went to the toilet and was gone too long he became agitated and upset awaiting my return, close to tears. It was so very different and frightening. Whereas before I had constantly been running around after him, and on many occasions been absolutely petrified because I had taken my eyes off of him for a moment and "lost" him, now I was in danger of walking on him, so close to my heels did he stay.

Of course both children were missing school so Nicky went to tell Mr D the situation. When he next came into the hospital, I asked how it had gone. He shook his head in disbelief and told me that when he had told him that Cole was in hospital, and had just been diagnosed with type 1 diabetes, Mr D's response was, "So when will they be back at school?" No sympathy, empathy, understanding, no asking how Cole was, nothing.

"What did you say?"

"Well, if I could find anything funny at the moment I would be laughing. I found myself talking to him like you see old people doing to foreigners: I raised my voice and spoke slowly, 'WE....DO....NOT....KNOW....NEITHER....DOES....THE....HOSPITAL,' and then I just turned on my heel and left because I did not trust myself not to punch him."

It did not bode well for when they did return.

So we learnt how to eat all over again. We learnt that some foods turned into sugar in the body and some did not, but the information given, while it seemed overwhelming at the time, I soon learnt was very basic. We were let out of the hospital after about five days knowing the following: we had to give Cole an injection of insulin in the morning, at about eight, and one in the evening, at about six; the insulin was a mixture of medium and slow-acting insulin, and to match the speed at which this insulin released into Cole's blood, he had to eat breakfast at 08:30, elevens' at 11:00, lunch at 13:00, afternoon snack at 16:00, tea at 18:30 and a bed time snack at 20:30. The times were only flexible by about 10-15 minutes. It was horrendous. We had never had a set time for any meal before, ever; it was always a moveable feast to suit whatever we were doing. He had never had to eat so much in all his life. In the beginning, Cole did not find it so difficult to eat at all these times as it was a novelty for him to be given so much extra food, but very shortly it lost its appeal as he realised that he had to eat even when he was not hungry; even his favourite food, roast dinners, became a chore to eat. We also knew that ideally we were aiming to keep Cole's glucose (sugar) levels in his blood between 4mmols (millimoles) and 10mmols, which proved to be virtually impossible. They were all over the place. Sometimes they were in the 20's and sometimes they were in the 2's! It was so scary. We were so afraid he would lapse into a coma when his readings were below 4mmols – he felt shaky and weak - that we would fire anything with sugar into him that he would take to bring his sugar levels up fast, and then followed it with something starchy to provide a slow release of sugar to stop him going low again. But we did not know how much of anything to give him, or how much time different sugary foods would take to have an effect, or what the insulin was doing. So in the beginning, in our terror, we would rocket his sugar levels way up, far too high, and then we would have to worry about getting them down again. It was one big, scary rollercoaster and we could not get off.

We went from a family who only ever had sweets and fizzy drinks in the house on special occasions, and maybe Saturday nights, to having them there permanently. Our wonderfully healthy diet seemed to have gone out the window in a shot. He ate vast amounts of starchy and sugary foods. If he went low in the middle of the night, and he did, often, we had to do the same, so he seemed to be permanently eating junk food. I had no idea what was happening, or what I was doing. It was all overwhelming and terrifying. We were afraid of sending him into a coma if he went too low – what the hell was too low? No one could tell us. He could become unconscious at 2mmols or lower, it depended on the child. If he did lapse into a coma would his brain be affected? Did it depend on how long he stayed in the coma, or how often it happened, or a combination of both? Again, it apparently depended on the child. We were afraid of highs as they too could induce a coma; though we knew that we had longer to respond in this case, that he would have to stay high for a while to go into a coma. Define "a while?" Guess what, it depends on the child. If "high," Cole would start to feel nauseous, have a headache and could become grouchy, but he rarely complained, so I did not always pick up on it as fast as I would have liked. Not only is there a risk of going into a coma if you go too high or too low, but poor control of your bloods (sugar levels) will lead to poor health later in life. Oh yes, and later in life can mean starting in your late teens! Poor health means anything from nerve damage (which can lead to gangrene and so to loss of limbs), to blindness, to heart attack, to mention but a few. And the best part? Every single thing was discussed within his hearing by the medical profession and everyone else. He was just eight years old and he had to face his own mortality; and the fact that if I screwed it up he could die now or earlier than he should.

One of the most heart-rending moments in my life was when we returned home from the hospital. Cole leapt out of the car and tore into the house. I knew why, and so walked in slowly after him, not wanting to witness what I knew was going to happen. You see, I knew that to him, home was a magic place where life was wonderful and fun and Mum and Dad could sort out anything. So I knew that, in his mind, all must surely be alright when he got home. I found him in the kitchen, curled up in a little ball in front of the AGA, (our range, which is the heart of the house). He did not cry, he did not shout or lash out. I would have preferred this; no he just lay there not talking to anyone, his little face blank and devoid of all hope and all I could do was sit down beside him and hold him.

So we tried to get back into as "normal" a life as possible. Though seriously, "normal" was so far removed from our vocabulary by now as to be laughable - a foreign concept. Cole and Ariana needed to return to school, but before this I went to the school to explain, as best as I could, what was happening to his teacher and our friend, Mr D. I explained the little I knew of Cole's diabetes and what he would need to do while at school to stay safe and alive. He would need to check his bloods (sugar levels) regularly. This would require sticking a needle into his finger and drawing blood which he then fed into a meter that would read his levels for him. He would also need to react to this information: if "low" he would have to eat or drink something; if "high" I would need to be called and come down and inject some insulin into him. The first thing we came up against was that his teacher said that Cole could not check his bloods in her class as she was afraid of blood. I explained that we were talking drops of blood, not gushing arteries, but to no avail. This was a problem, Cole needed to check his bloods in school at break and lunch time always and if he felt "funny" to see if he was too "high" (hyperglycaemia) or too "low" (hypoglycaemia), so that he could respond appropriately. So it was agreed that he would step out into the corridor, that from the start Ariana would be allowed to leave her classroom to be with him should he need help, and that they could call me if they needed help. Cole and Ariana now both had mobile phones so that they could contact me should Cole need help. The irony of this was not lost on me. Only a month previously, if the children had wanted a mobile phone I would have laughed and told them "good try" but no, they could not have one as they did not need it and that the radio waves that they emitted were not, in my opinion, good for anyone's brain and especially a child's. Now it seemed the lesser of two evils to have a phone and risk the long term exposure to the waves, rather than us all being terrified by the thought of Cole not being able to call us for help, and all the horrifying scenarios that this would conjure up.

The next issue that arose was that if Cole lapsed into a coma from going too "low", he would need an injection of glucose (sugar) to bring his bloods back up as he would not be able to eat or drink. This would need to be administered immediately to bring him out of the coma. The teachers flatly refused to do this, saying that their insurance would not cover it. They would call me, Nicky, or the doctor's surgery if they could not get us. On hearing this, Cole was distraught, who would save him if he went too low and into a coma? Ariana, my wonderful ten year old, who was struggling with her own challenges, but who loved her brother dearly, stepped into the breach. She had me show her what to do with the injection and we practised on an orange. So Cole's life line during school hours was his ten-year-old sister, not an adult.

So we lurched from one episode to another, slowly learning what to do along the way.

Right from the beginning, I realised that the sooner Cole could give himself his own injections, the sooner he would regain some of his independence. This was another really stinky moment in our lives. I would happily have given his injections to him forever, as I would have done anything to make his life easier, but I knew that that was not, in the long term, going to help him. Would he want me turning up at school every time he needed to inject insulin because he was "high?" No. When he went to friends' houses, would he want me to have to go with him, or arrive at meal times, or if he went "high," to administer the insulin? Of course not. In fact, did he want to be carting me around, everywhere he went, like some extra appendage? No, of course not. So while he was still reeling from all the horror that was now his life, and while I felt like a complete heel, I bribed him to start doing his own injections. I told him that I would buy him the biggest transformer in the toy shop if he would do his injections, himself, for a week and explained why I thought he needed to start doing them.

He listened to me and then looked at me with a face devoid of joy and said, "I will do them, but I do not want anything."

"Why not?"

"It won't change anything. I am going to have to do them anyway if I want to go anywhere without you. So you do not have to buy me anything, Mum. I know this is the way it has to be."

Then both he and I cried, hugged each other tightly and tried to get on with our lives.

Very shortly after the children returned to school, Mr D decided that I was again an over protective mother. His reasoning this time was that Cole had become too dependent on me. I took a deep breath when he said this to me and explained that Cole's dependency on me was because he was afraid of dying that he knew that no teacher in school would give him the life-saving injection should he need it, and that he was therefore afraid of leaving me. But no, according to Mr D and Cole's teacher, it was because I was mollycoddling him. When I asked them on what they were basing this, they could only come up with the example of me carrying his bag into school for him each day. That was their sole evidence of my mollycoddling him. They informed me that from now on I was not to be allowed to enter the school building. I asked them how they were going to know what was happening with Cole's bloods each morning if I was not to come in?

"Send in a note."

"If I were to write on a note that Cole's bloods were 4mmols or 24mmols, would you know what that meant and how to respond appropriately?" I asked.

They admitted that no, actually, it would mean nothing to them, and so I was to write an explanation on the note! I tried to argue that this was cruel and irresponsible beyond words, but they were immovable. I had to leave because I was afraid that if I stayed I would leap across the desk and rip their eyes out. That morning, on waking, I had not thought that I could have felt more desperate, sad or disillusioned with humanity. It turned out that I had been sadly mistaken; life could indeed get harder.

# Chapter 8

So Ariana struggled with school still, but managed to go because she and Cole both knew that she was the only one who cared enough about him to look out for him. There was one other lovely little girl in his class who cared. She would meet me every day and say, "Cole's bloods were X, was that OK?" She would also ask what else he should be doing and remind him to do so. Thus it was down to Cole and Ariana and this little friend - two eight year olds and a 10 year old – without any adult help, to watch out for him and to try and keep him alive in my absence. Life sure wasn't a bed of roses. Silly us, we had expected support and help from society. How naive of us. "Help" was apparently only available if you stayed within what was deemed "normal" parameters. As we had found out with Ariana, if you did not fit in the box, then it must be something that you were doing wrong. So all your own fault; in fact, probably deserved. Therefore those who were in a position to help, such as teachers or medical professionals, were completely exonerated from having to think outside of the box and look for a way to help a child on an individual basis.

The school year was almost at a close, so we just hung in there and hoped that things would improve come September.

During that summer we tried hard to just have fun and to find "normal" again; something I have since come to realise will never again exist for any of us. I took the children in our campervan to visit a friend and her children in the north of Ireland. One day we drove, her in her car and me in the campervan, to the Giant's Causeway as my children had never seen it. On arriving, Théa and Cole leapt out and took off with our friend and her children. Before I could blink, they had all headed off on the walk down to the causeway. Ariana and I raced after them. Half way down I suddenly stopped dead in my tracks. I had realised that I had come without any food for Cole if his sugar levels went low and that I had no way of knowing what his sugar levels were anyway because I had also forgotten the meter! They were all back in the van. I felt as if the blood was draining out of my body from the top down. I went completely cold. Did I go back to get them? I was already about 10 minutes behind them as it was. If I went back I would not be with Cole for another 45 minutes! Anything could have happened in that time; he could be unconscious and I would not be there! I raced on down with Ariana running to keep up with me, while I prayed to that non-existent sadistic sod, God, "Please, please, keep my baby conscious, let me get there and let him be alright. Let me be in time."

We found them all dancing along the rocks that make up the Giant's Causeway having a wonderful time and I started to breathe again, though I knew we were far from safe yet. As fast as I could I started to head back up to the van with Cole. My friend did not realise how scared I was. She had no idea what I was feeling or any way of knowing what I feared. She knew nothing of diabetes, while I knew so little I could not explain rationally why I was so terrified. Even if I could have, I did not want to freak Cole out. All she knew was that I was behaving in the most irrational manner, and having gone out of her way to facilitate us, I must have appeared to be most ungrateful. On the way back, Cole started to slow down, Ariana and I slowed with him, but the others, unaware of anything being wrong, went on ahead.

Suddenly Cole stopped and said, "Mum, I feel really funny. I cannot walk anymore. My legs feel really shaky and it's hard to stand."

We stopped and he sat down for a few minutes, but all that happened was that he began to feel worse; all his symptoms intensified. I tried to give him a piggy back, but as he weighed 50 odd kilos I only made it a very short distance before I had to stop. For those of you who have not been to the Giant's Causeway, it is a magnificent and awe-inspiring place, but the distance from the car park to the bottom is about a half hour stroll and on the way back it is all uphill. The only vehicles allowed down are the Causeway's own coaches and these you need to access at the top or bottom. The children sat down, both now white with fear. Then I saw a coach setting off from the bottom on its return to the top. I stood in the middle of the road with my hand out, in the stop position, like King Canute who had tried to stop the tide. As she got nearer to me, the driver waved madly for me to get out of the way and beeped her horn. Ariana asked "What if she doesn't stop?"

"She will have to, or drive over me and use me for grip," I replied.

The driver stopped about 10 feet away from me gesticulating wildly, and glaring formidably. I knew that if I took one step to the side she would gun the engine and speed on past us, so I walked right up to the front of the bus and when I stepped around to the door, I was so close that she would have had to drive over my feet to continue. She yelled through the door that this was a private tour and that I could not get on the bus. I am not surprised that she did not open the door: I must have looked extremely wild eyed and as if I was on drugs by this stage; rather frightening. I yelled back through the door, "It is an emergency, please open the door. My child has diabetes and he is sick. We have to get back to the top immediately."

We were mortified at the scene we were making and the attention that we were drawing to ourselves, but our fear of Cole lapsing into a coma was greater. It was then that the bus driver saw the children, and looking at their terrified, young faces she immediately opened the door. Ariana and I half lifted, half dragged Cole onto the bus, thanking the driver at the same time. She immediately sped up to the car park where we again supported Cole back to the campervan. When we got there, Ariana immediately got Cole some apple juice to drink as it was all that we had. We had yet to realise that we needed to behave like Coca-Cola addicts, religiously having some with us at all times.

"I cannot drink, my mouth does not want to work properly," Cole slurred.

"Cole, if you cannot drink this I am going to have to give you the glucose injection, and you know how big that needle is, don't you?"

It was as if I was looking at someone with hypothermia. His mouth was moving only slightly and his words were dribbling out of it. I knew that he was terrified of that needle, and so even though I felt like a creep threatening him with it, it worked and he started to sip the juice while I supported him and held the cup to his mouth. We checked his bloods and gave him more juice. After about ten to fifteen minutes, he started to speak properly again. By this time Théa had arrived back, taken one look at the situation, and started to get some food together for Cole to eat. At this time, we had no idea what we were doing, only that he had too much insulin in his system and not enough food, so we just fed him till his sugars came back up and he felt better. Stabbing his finger to check his bloods every 15 minutes until we were "happy" again with his levels. It invariably meant that later he would be too high because we had over fed him, and that he would then have to give himself several injections, of small amounts of insulin, over a period of several hours to balance this. It was a yo-yo effect.

So the summer went by. We had some fun and we had some of the most hair-raising crazy moments that we had ever experienced in our lives. When we were on holidays that year in Connemara, I went into town to get the groceries, leaving Cole with Nicky. The next door neighbour had just bought a beautiful shiny new power boat, and knowing that Nicky had experience both with engines and boats, asked Nicky if he would come out with him for a spin to make sure that all was as it should be. Nicky jumped at the chance to "have a go" of this new shiny boy toy and stuffed Cole and his friend into their lifejackets. In minutes they were all in the boat and heading out to sea on a wonderful adventure, with the children laughing with glee at the speed of the boat and the thought of being able to say they had been in it to the rest of us later. They went to an island off the shore where the lighthouse was stationed and while cruising around it, the engine got fouled in some rope that was floating below the surface of the water. Nicky, unfazed, freed the engine and restarted it, only to find that it did not want to restart. Not particularly bothered by this development, Nicky threw out the anchor to stop them from drifting on to the rocks and started to work out the problem. It was a lovely sunny day and all were confident that Nicky would soon know what the issue was. Then Cole said, "Dad I feel funny."

Nicky looked at his son and went cold with shock and fear. In his eagerness to play with the new boat, he had forgotten to bring Cole's bag containing his meter, insulin and any food to treat a "low." Telling Cole not to worry, that they would soon be back at the house, he now returned to the problem of starting the engine with a previously unfelt sense of urgency and fear, all the while wondering how "low" Cole was. Was he going to collapse into a coma at any moment? He had no way of knowing. After what seemed like ages, but was in fact only five minutes or so, he had the engine restarted. Turning to our neighbour, he quietly said that he needed to get Cole back to the house as soon as possible and so needed to drive the boat at full speed. The neighbour had obviously picked up Nicky's sense of urgency and readily agreed. So with everyone holding on tight, he floored the engine and tore back to the house. All later agreed that the return ride was not fun. In fact, it was so uncomfortable bouncing across the top of the waves that Cole's friend was almost in tears by the time their short journey was completed. Nicky abandoned neighbour and boat, picked up the two children and ran up the short distance to the house. By the time I returned, it was all over. Well, mostly over. Cole and his friend were playing again and Cole was no longer "low." Nicky, having had no idea how much to feed him to bring his sugars back up, had basically opened any, and every sweet food or drink that he could find and let the children loose. Cole, out of fear and ravenous hunger in the beginning, had eaten masses, but then joining his friend in her obvious delight at such unexpected good fortune, had continued to eat until both had felt slightly ill. It looked as if there had been a wild party, with wrappers and containers all over the place. I was so thankful that Cole was alright and not drifting in a coma somewhere out at sea, and Nicky was so obviously shaken by the whole episode, that I did not have the heart to point out to him that it would take me hours to sort out the high that was going to follow that amount of sugar.

We lived in a state of constant alert, never fully relaxed, always trying to anticipate how different situations would affect Cole. I started to do more and more research on the "internet" - a new and most remarkable tool that we could now access from our home computer. It was, however, remarkably slow as we had to plug the computer into the phone line and laboriously download information.

One of the first things that I checked out was something called the Somogyi effect. We had been told by the hospital that there was no need for us to get up and test Cole's bloods during the night as the "Somogyi effect" would always catch any "lows" that he had when asleep, causing his body to release glucose from his liver, and in so doing raise him back up to a safe or higher than normal level, which was preferable to low, but absolutely no reason to worry. Well, as worry was now my newest best friend, whom I hated, it was pointless to say not to worry. Right from the start I could not see the logic in this "Somogyi effect." I mean, if we had to treat "lows" during the day because his body was unable to sort them out, why would it be any different at night just because the body was sleeping? I would see Cole go "low" during the day and sometimes not be aware of it until he was in and around 2 mmol. There is not much lower than 2 to go numerically. Once, he had even been in and around 1 mmol. What if he went off the scale? Obviously, we had the risk of him going into a coma, but was it possible that if he went "low" during the night and did not wake/respond, he could die? Also, as I had no idea how the insulin he injected was responding – how many hours intermediate insulin and long term insulin each lasted in the body, whether they released/worked at a steady constant rate and then suddenly ended or whether their effectiveness dropped by a percentage each hour – I had no idea if he was going to bed with a lot of active working insulin, which, if he went low, could drive him even lower. Then there was the fact that I did not know what affected insulin's efficiency. Was it just the amount of food you ate? Or was it, as I was beginning to suspect, many factors such as how much he exercised, if he was sick, if he was growing? It made absolutely no sense to me at all that if Cole could go "low" during the day and need to be treated, that the same would not also be true at night.

So I looked up the Somogyi effect and was horrified to find out that it was a theoretical phenomenon that Dr Michael Somogyi had hypothesized about somewhere around 1938, over sixty years earlier. I was unable to find any evidence that anyone had tried to prove this hypothesis since. I also found out that a lot of parents believed that their child, when "low" during the night, did not wake up by themselves; and worst of all, that some parents actually believed that because their child had gone "low" and not been able to wake up that they had died. So, as far as I could see, the hospital were asking me to bet the life of my child on an "unproven theory" that had been suggested over half a century earlier! Not happening, no way. I needed to know more. So I started to check on Cole's bloods during the night. I started by doing it about three hours after he had gone to sleep, and then three hours later, then three hours later again. I found that sometimes when I checked him he could be in the 2's, and not only had he not woken, but I found it extremely hard to rouse him at all. Sometimes, as I shook him vigorously and called his name in ever increasing volume, I would think that if anyone could see me doing this they would report me for child cruelty, and wasn't it a good thing he was not a baby or I would be locked up for shaken baby syndrome. So if he was "low," I would wake him and feed him – we called them our "midnight picnics" – then I would climb into bed beside him and check his bloods after 15 minutes and then again every subsequent 15 minutes, until I was sure that they had risen to, and were maintaining, a "safe" level.

One of the hardest things was that the next day, (because this happened a lot in the beginning it was most days), everyone else outside of the household expected us to function as "normal". I began to hate that word, "normal." They expected Cole to perform well at school; they expected us to happily fit in like everyone else. We were barely surviving. I was more sleep deprived than I had been when the children were newborns, as not only was I checking Cole's bloods during the night, but Ariana was still so unhappy that she was not sleeping soundly through the nights but waking and looking for reassurance and comfort. And I was supposed to function as before and get everyone to school on time. No one made any allowances at the school. In fact, they always had an opinion, along with many other people, on how lousy a job I was doing. We rarely went anywhere because no one (except my parents) could understand that dinner now had to be at a certain time, no exceptions, and because we had always had such a bohemian attitude towards food and life before, many people were actually cross with us and felt we were being hypocritical and fussy. Fussy!

# Chapter 9

I also stopped going down to our local village. I would rather drive to the next village, where no one knew me, than go to the local shop and risk meeting someone who did. The reason for this was that I was discovering that people do one of two things when they meet you after some major upheaval has happened to you in life.

The first scenario was that they met me and said, "I heard that Cole was diagnosed with diabetes. How are you?"

I quickly realised that what they wanted me to say was "fine," or "oh, things are hard" and stop there. They did not want me to elaborate. They did not want to know that I was about to lose the plot because I was beyond tired, or that I was sick in my stomach with fear most of the time, especially when I had to let him out of my sight. They could not handle my pain or fear or despair; it made them feel uncomfortable. I know this because in the beginning I was foolish enough to try to explain to some people how I really was. They would start to shift from foot to foot, or their eyes would slide away from me, and suddenly they would remember that they had forgotten that they needed to be somewhere else.

The second scenario would be that when they met me they would offer some sort of platitude because it made them feel better. Again, nothing to do with me. Some of the platitudes were like the following: "I heard Cole was diagnosed with diabetes. Well, aren't you lucky that it was not cancer?"

For some reason they seemed to think that this had not crossed my mind. It was one of the first things that had crossed my mind, and of course I was grateful that he did not have cancer, but it did not make life miraculously better. It did not take away my fear of him dying early or because of something I did or did not do right. And it did not make it any easier to watch his pain.

Or

"I heard about Cole, so lucky that he got it now while he was young and not when he was a teenager when he would have rebelled."

"Lucky!" Where was the luck in any of this? "Lucky" would have been never to have it. And of course he was still going to rebel as a teenager. What teenager does not rebel? He would now just have more than most to rebel against and more for me to worry about.

Or

"Oh yes, my aunt had diabetes and she had to have her leg amputated."

Sadly, many people told me horror stories about relatives with diabetes. In the beginning, I was so stunned that they were actually telling me these things that I did not know how to react. I wish I had either walked away or asked, "While that is extremely sad for your aunt, how does telling me this story help me or Cole?"

Or

"Well he'll soon get used to it."

Used to it! I'd like to see them getting used to always sticking needles into themselves or never being able to eat spontaneously ever again.

Two of the worst things that were often offered were: "It's alright; God never gives anyone more than they can bear." As far as I was concerned, God, if indeed there was a God, was having a laugh and just waiting to see when and how spectacular a spectacle I would make when I crashed and burned.

Or

"What doesn't kill us makes us stronger."

This would bring a rage up inside of me that I had never in my life experienced before. I thought I would kill someone. I wanted to leap across the few feet that separated us and beat them to within an inch of their lives and then say to them, "Well, God thought you were looking a bit weak lately and he wished to make you stronger, so, you know, 'What does not kill you makes you stronger,' just remember that while you get better" and "It'll be alright you know, He never gives you more than you can bear!"

They had absolutely no idea, not a clue.

# Chapter 10

When the children returned to school it soon became obvious that nothing had changed. Ariana still struggled with being there and interpreting everyone's behaviour, and Cole was still treated with a complete lack of care. Just before Halloween, Ariana stood outside the school door, straightened her back and turned around to me and said, in a calm and mature voice, "Mum, I cannot do this anymore. I am never going back into this place ever again," then she turned and walked slowly and deliberately back to the car and got in. She was just 11 years old.

I was amazed. Part of me wanted to applaud her and yell, "Way to go girl!" as she had been so mature and decisive. Another part of me was going, "Oh rats, oh rats, what am I going to do now?"

Cole had already gone into class when Ariana delivered her bombshell. When he called me at break time with his bloods, he of course asked where Ariana was, so I told him that she was with me and asked if he thought he could manage on his own that day. While he did this, and did it well, I was terrified. Over the next few days, Cole went to school on his own, his choice, not mine, while Nicky and I tried to find a solution to help Ariana.

In the end, help came from a most unexpected source. Out of sheer desperation we went to the local parish priest which seems the oddest thing for us to have done, as we are not Catholic. However, in the Irish national school system, technically the parish priest is the head of the school board, and as I was not getting anywhere with the principal this seemed the next step to take. By this stage I did not know if I even believed in God. Certainly, I hated him if he did exist and I had no faith in any religious system, but as I have come to realise over the years, it is the individual that matters, not the system that he or she represents. The individual, if they choose to live in a way that is for the higher good of all, can make all the difference regardless of the system they find themselves in. This particular Catholic priest made a huge difference to us, even though we were not part of his group, and we were saying that the school that he was part of was failing our children.

He was the first person in the "system" to listen to me, and hear what I was saying. The first thing he said was, "This is very serious. Ariana needs help as she is a very sad little child and I am worried for her. Perhaps this particular type of school system does not suit her; I do not believe that it is for everyone. There is a school just opened a little bit from here. It is a Steiner school. I know nothing about it at all but it might be worth you looking into it. If you decide that you wish to try the local school some more, I will certainly visit Ariana at school and see if I can help her. But I am not sure of how much help I can be to her."

The gratitude I felt towards this man was immense. He was the first person who realised that Ariana was struggling and desperate and he did not once suggest or imply that we were to blame. He thought outside of the box and just looked for a way to help us. We thanked him for his kindness, though it was impossible to convey to him how much it meant to us, and left. The minute I got home I searched on the internet for this "Steiner" school. I found a reference to it in an old newspaper article and phoned the number given and, after a few phone calls, I had the number of the school. I called them and left a message on the voicemail. That day they called me and we made an appointment to go and meet them. They asked that the children come too as, they pointed out, this was about them after all.

At the meeting we met the teachers of both Cole's and Ariana's years and the principal and, while they talked with Nicky and myself, they also talked directly to the children and explained how things were run in this school.

I explained how things were for Ariana, and about Cole's diabetes. It turned out that the teacher of Cole's year had type 1 diabetes too! So if we did move the children to this school there would be no squeamishness about blood, someone would give the glucose injection to him if he went into a coma and they would know what I meant when I told them what his bloods were! Also, the teacher in Ariana's year turned around to her and said, "If you do not understand anything that I have said in class or told you to do, then it means that I have not explained it properly and you are to ask me to explain it again."

Hallelujah! Adults who actually cared about children as individuals. We asked if the children could come to this school, right there and then, we did not need any time to think about it. Who cared about the 40 minute commute each way if they had a chance of being happy, safe and listened to? They said that they would need to look into the feasibility of it, as there were quite a few children wishing to join at the moment and, while there were quite a few places in one of the classrooms, the other really was quite full. We went home, Nicky and I fervently wishing that they would be able to take our children. They actually called later that day, about an hour after we got home, to say that after we had left they had all agreed unanimously that our children were in desperate need of their help and care and that they could start with them after the Halloween break. The relief was immense.

Right from the start the Steiner school system accommodated both the children's needs. Cole's teacher was happy for me to discuss Cole's needs with him, to tell me if he felt that Cole needed help in anything and to let me know in advance if they were doing anything out of the ordinary, such as any form of exercise or trips, so that I could plan in advance on the best strategies to try and keep his bloods within safe levels. Cole knew he was safe and cared for and that the teachers would always look after him and contact me should he need me. Being the easy child he was, he made friends quickly and enjoyed the way in which subjects were taught through actions, stories and the participation of the students and teachers together. He started to become more independent again. Ariana's fears about being separated from me and her inability to "read" people were handled with love and compassion. The teachers told Ariana that if she needed to call me she would be allowed do so, preferably at break times, that they would always listen to her if she wished to say something to them, and would be happy to explain things to her if she did not understand. Having been lied to in her previous school, as far as she was concerned, where teachers said one thing and did another, Ariana did not believe them at first. But as time went by they kept their promises and she began to trust them. Ariana, while still not able to interpret people, their actions or their reasons for doing things, at least felt safe in the knowledge that the teachers would call me if needed and would listen to her and explain things again to her, in different ways, until she understood. Monumentally, by the end of the year, Ariana was able to sleep all night again, every night, in her own room.

The compassion shown to us by these teachers and the Steiner system itself made a huge difference to our lives and to our family. While we still had huge challenges, I could at least know that when the children were in school they were cared for and loved.

# Chapter 11

With no outside help, and not knowing anyone who was remotely going through what we were, I threw myself into research. It quite literally kept me sane and gave me some hope. I also realised that it was up to me; no one else was going to rescue us; there was no knight in shining armour galloping in to save me. I was on my own. Sink or swim. And I did almost sink many times over the coming years. The one thing that kept me going was the knowledge that I could not fail my children, it was just something that I was incapable of letting happen, an inbuilt fail safe mechanism that seemed to drag me back from the edge of the abyss each time, even if it did seem not to kick in till the very last minute at times!

So now that Ariana and Cole were attending a school that treated them on an individual basis and actively encouraged them in thinking for themselves while caring enough about their well-being to listen to their needs, I was able to try to find information that might be of help to us, that might actually allow us to pull ourselves out of this nightmare.

There were several things that I wanted to know at this time.

What caused autism? Because I now believed that, no matter what anyone else said, that Ariana was exhibiting traits that were definitely associated with autism. I also knew that she had been just fine in early childhood and had changed slowly after one set of vaccinations and then monumentally after another, was there a link? Were there other causes? Was anyone looking for causes?

What could be done to cure it?

What caused type 1 diabetes? Because, in Cole's case, it was not anything to do with genetics, there was no history of it in either side of the family.

What was the best method of managing it?

Had I played a part in causing either of these health challenges? Was it my fault?

What I found was startling. No one knew for sure what caused autism or type 1 diabetes. Lots of theories were being offered and, while there was a lot of time and money being spent on looking at ways to "cure" type 1 diabetes and to manage it better, no money, that I could see, was being spent on looking for the causes of either conditions.

Again, I kept coming across parents and some doctors who questioned the safety of vaccines. I struggled with this one, as I had been brought up to believe that vaccines were not only safe but necessary. Everyone I knew had been vaccinated, including myself. However, now that I had seen Ariana become a totally different child, a changeling, within a week of having a vaccination, I could not ignore the evidence of my own eyes that the two were related. Believe me though, when I say that I did want to ignore it, I wanted to shut my eyes, screw them up, shake my head and open them again to find that all was as it had been before. But I could not, life was hell, and the voice inside my head was screaming at me to look into vaccines and their safety. But what if I found that the safety was questionable? Then it would mean that I would have no choice but to face the fact that I had, albeit unintentionally, harmed my children and I would have to live with the guilt that would come with that knowledge forever. But I could no longer put it off, so I started looking.

I had always been under the impression that vaccines were made up of the actual "disease," such as measles, mumps and rubella in the MMR and little else, perhaps just sterile water? I now found out that I was very much mistaken. In fact, vaccines can have many ingredients, such as mercury (called thimerosal), aluminium, formaldehyde, animal tissue, animal blood, human blood, human cells from aborted babies, potato starch, yeast, lactose, phenol, antibiotics and the odd germ or two that inadvertently get into the vaccine culture! These additives are apparently used as preservatives or adjuvants. Adjuvants are substances that are used to trigger the body's immune response to the "disease" (antigen) in the vaccine. So what about these preservatives and adjuvants, were they safe?

We all stopped using aluminium saucepans when I was growing up in the 1980s because we had been told by the scientists that aluminium was a possible cause to Alzheimer's. So I started by looking at that, and discovered that more than 10 years later (and still true of today), aluminium was still being put into vaccines. How could that possibly make sense? If it is not safe to eat food that has been cooked in an aluminium pot, how can it possibly be safe to inject aluminium into our bodies? Were there minimal amounts that someone thought "safe" to inject into babies? Yes, the European Food Safety Association (EFSA) says that a dietary intake (what one can eat in your food) of 1mg of aluminium, per kg of body weight, per week is acceptable (EFSA, 2008). So a baby weighing 10kg (an average 6 month old) can eat food with 10mg of aluminium in it per week, but out of this 10mg only 3% of it (0.3mg) is actually absorbed into the body; the rest travels from the mouth to the anus and is excreted out of the body. So the amount of aluminium that is allowed to enter the blood and system of that 10kg baby per week is 0.3mg. Yet one vaccine can contain 0.85mg of aluminium, 2.5 times the allowable amount. So just think how much greater the ratio is for a baby of one or two months? Not only that, but that baby is not just getting one vaccine but multiple vaccines at one time, so could be getting as much as 1000mg in one day! (Gunn, 2011)

Formaldehyde, I soon found out, is used as an embalming fluid for the dead! Mercury, aluminium and formaldehyde are all neurotoxins, which means that they are poisonous to the brain. They kill brain cells, something that most parents, funnily enough, want to keep alive in their children.

By now my mind was reeling. So many questions kept popping up. Who decided on what the "safe" upper limits of ingredients like aluminium were that are put into vaccines? And how had they established these "safe" limits?

It would appear that no one knows, as is highlighted by the following extract from Trevor Gunn's (a medical biochemist) book *Vaccines – This book could remove the fear of childhood illness.*

> *In the transcript from the National Vaccine Program Office Workshop on Aluminium in Vaccines, May 2000, Dr Gerber, National Institute of Health asks the following question:*
>
> *"...the standard of 0.85milligrams of aluminium per dose set forth in the Code of Federal Regulations, can you tell us where that came from and how that was determined?"*
>
> *Dr Baylor, Acting Deputy Director of the Office of Vaccine Research and Review, and Associate Director for Regulatory Policy at the Centre for Biological Evaluation of Research at FDA (Food and Drugs Administration) replies:*
>
> *"Unfortunately, I could not. I mean, we have been trying to figure that out. We have been trying to figure that out as far as going back in the historical records and determining how they came up with that and going back to the preamble to the regulation. We just have been unsuccessful with that but we are still trying to figure that out."*
>
> *In the same meeting Dr Martin Myers, Director of the National Vaccine Programme Office, Department of Health and Human Services states:*

*"Perhaps the most important thing that I took away from the last meeting was that those of us who deal with vaccines have really very little applicable background with metals and toxicological research."* (Gunn, 2011)

This was looking scarier by the minute. I had given my children vaccines which my doctor believed were safe. Yet those same vaccines were now hugely questionable in my eyes, as it became obvious that those doctors in charge of vaccine safety and research, and vaccine programmes did not know how "safe" levels for a neurotoxin in vaccines was determined and when!

So if the safe levels of the ingredients in vaccines are questionable, how can vaccines pass their safety evaluations?

Well it seems that they do not! No, I am not joking, read on and you can see for yourself. In his introduction to Catherine J Frompovich's book, and *Vaccination Voodoo – What YOU Don't Know About Vaccines* (Frompovich, 2013), Paul G King, PhD tells us that:

*"To establish that a vaccine preservative is "nontoxic", scientifically sound and appropriate, toxicological studies must be conducted that prove that that dose of preservative in a vaccine is not toxic to the most susceptible individual to which that vaccine may be given. To do this, the toxicity studies must establish the "no observed adverse effect level" (NOAEL) for the most susceptible system in humans using chronic toxicity studies in an animal model from which the proper most-susceptible human toxicity thresholds (NOAELs) can be reliable computed.*

*However, though required to do so since 1968, when the National Institutes of Health (NIH) regulated vaccines, and since 1973, when the United States Congress transferred the regulation of vaccines to the FDA, and subsequently required the manufacturers to submit all required proofs of safety to the FDA since 1999, the vaccine makers have refused to establish the NOAEL values for Thimerosal-preserved vaccines in the developing human, pregnant woman, adult and/or elderly person to whom these vaccines may be repeatedly administered and, contrary to law since 1977, the FDA has licensed these Thimerosal-preserved vaccines delivering 15 to 50 micrograms of Thimerosal per vaccine dose."* (Frompovich, 2013)

So it appeared to me that there were, and still are, no studies establishing the safety of the preservatives and adjuvants in vaccines. In fact, because these studies have not been done, as required by law, vaccines cannot meet any safety guidelines. Yet they are still "approved" by the FDA and the EFSA. It begs the question, "Why?" And also raises questions such as, "How come my doctor did not know this? Where was he getting his information from?"

So where do doctors get their information on drugs and vaccines from? Well, the answer is frighteningly simple. They get the information from the manufacturers of those drugs and vaccines. Oh, there are studies on the drugs and vaccines, but all those studies are either directly or indirectly linked to the pharmaceutical companies who made them. Wow! That was hard to believe, and yet I really did search hard for independent research that had been carried out on vaccines that showed without doubt that they were safe and effective, and I could not find any. If the manufacturer had not directly paid for the research, then the university or institute that carried out that research, accepted money from the manufacturer to fund other research, or positions within the establishment, or new buildings. Or the researchers themselves were linked to the drug companies by various means such as shares or previous payments. Then the research was written up in medical journals either by a researcher, but often by someone employed by the drug company called a "ghost writer." Then the company paid a doctor to put his name to the article! Lastly, everyone's doctor read the article in the respected medical journal, believed it without question, as it was apparently "peer-reviewed", and was happy to prescribe the described drug or vaccine to their patients.

The definition of "bias" in the New Oxford Dictionary of English is, *"prejudice in favour of or against one thing, person, or group compared with another, especially in a way considered to be unfair."* (New Oxford Dictionary, 1998) Well, if someone is paying your wages, or funding your research or facility, you will be biased by default because they can pull the plug on your financial security at any moment should they not like what you report.

An example of this bias can be seen by looking at what happened in England in 2001. The UK health authority publicised a Finnish report, citing it as proof that the MMR vaccine did not cause autism. However, this report was supported by a grant from one of the manufacturers of the MMR vaccine, Merck & Co, USA; the documents which were written about this report and distributed to doctors were written by one of the medical directors of Aventis Pasteur, also a manufacturer of a MMR vaccine. Not only was there bias, but the report did not even look for symptoms of autism! It looked for reactions such as fits, allergies, neurological disorders, rheumatoid arthritis and diabetes and was concentrated on the three week period after the vaccination was given, so it missed the appearance of any of the symptoms associated with regressive autism. (Gunn, 2011)

I felt as if I had fallen into Alice's "wonderland." How could all this possibly be true? Everything that I had believed in, the "safety" of medicines, the belief that my doctor "knew" all about those drugs, the belief that there was a "policing" system in place to make sure that all drugs were "safe," was shot to hell. I realised that I had been incredibly naive and foolish to believe without question that drugs/vaccines were safe and that doctors did research for themselves. The only information that I had ever received about vaccines had been either by word of mouth from my doctor, or in the form of a glossy government flier. How odd was that? Very, considering that if I bought an over the counter medication there was always a manufacturer's information leaflet with it, required by law, listing any known side effects of that drug. Yet the only thing I had ever been told would be the side effect of a vaccine was a mild rash or temperature and that my child may be out of sorts for a while. Now I was finding that, not only was there a question as to whether vaccines were connected to autism, but there was also a question as to whether they were related to Sudden Infant Death Syndrome (SIDS) and many other childhood diseases such as asthma, allergies, eczema and, of particular interest to me, type 1 diabetes.

In 1997, Harris Coulter, Ph.D, presented a paper before the Congress of the United States in which he says:

> *"While researchers are well aware of the significance of vaccinations as etiological agents in the production of diabetes, the Public Health service and related agencies promoting vaccination programs deny or ignore this relationship or are simply unaware of it. At any rate, the public is not yet being informed of this additional and very real risk from the vaccines which they are compelled to administer to their children.*
>
> *"The seriousness of Type-1 diabetes is perhaps not appreciated by the public at large. While not quite a death sentence, it is close to it. Panzram wrote in 1984: "Type-1 diabetes, particularly at a young age, must be considered as a rather serious disease, with a 5 to 10-fold higher excess in mortality in comparison with the general population." Diabetes is the seventh leading cause of death in the United States. Type-1, especially, means a shortened life with many disagreeable features such as stroke, kidney failure, cardiovascular complications, blindness and the need to amputate gangrenous limbs."*

He also says:

> *"No Investigation of the Vaccine Connection – As we will see, while there is much circumstantial and "anecdotal" evidence (meaning case histories) in favor of a diabetes/vaccination*

*connection, this has never been officially investigated, the fact that the federal medical establishment – which would be the major source of funds for such an epidemiologic investigation – is itself highly committed to the childhood vaccination program, goes far to explain the absence of any official interest in the connection. This is a major disadvantage of all research on damage from the childhood vaccination program. In fact, several of the vaccines administered for the diseases of childhood have been implicated in the causation of diabetes.* " (Coulter, 1997)

I was overwhelmed. I could not take it all in. Everything, and I mean everything, that I had taken for granted and believed in when it came to doctors and medicines was now in question. I stopped looking. I could not handle it. I could not believe it or accept it. I could not, and did not, want to know anymore. I was overwhelmed by so many emotions. Guilt, that I had never researched any of this prior to allowing my children to be given vaccinations. How could I not have looked into it? If I was buying a house, would I have just believed the auctioneer that the house was sound? No, I would have sought out an independent view. If I was buying a car, would I have just believed the salesman? No, I would have done my own research. For crying out loud, if I was buying a washing machine I would have researched it more! Yet I had allowed toxic, brain altering, morally questionable (remember the DNA from human foetuses and other species?) poison to be injected into my babies. Depression, that I, and so many others, were being misled, and that we were so trusting that we never thought to question the information given to us and ask where it had come from. And rage. Rage started to trickle slowly through me and build up into a torrent that threatened to engulf me. Rage, with myself for being so naive, but also with those that had told me categorically that vaccinations were, without question, safe. Where were those people now when my children were suffering and life was so tough? Nowhere. Absolutely no one was beating a path to our door to offer us any help.

So I took a break from looking at possible causes and totally shelved the horrendous notion that I may have hurt my children, I decided to focus on learning more about type 1 diabetes and its management, because I was sure that I must be able to do more for Cole. I was absolutely positive that I could help make Cole's life easier while keeping him as healthy as I possibly could. I could not, and would not, believe otherwise, even though that is exactly what we were being told. You see, not only did people in the street seem to delight in telling me about their aunt Mildred who had had to have her right foot and left arm amputated due to her diabetes, but the medical profession were also talking in front of Cole about the long term effects of poor control of one's diabetes. I realise that they wished us to understand right from the start that if we were not active in our management of Cole's diabetes that his health would suffer, but I have to say that they were sadly lacking in bedside manner in their delivery of this information. Cole was just eight years old, and suddenly he was not only having to inject himself several times a day, but also he was hearing that if we/he got it wrong he could go into a coma, possibly imminently as we had no idea what we were doing, and that he could look forward to the very real possibility of; losing his sight, nerve damage, ulcers, loss of limbs and heart attacks to name but a few, in the near future, not when he was old and grey. And the worst of this was that there was an air of inevitability about the whole thing, a foregone conclusion that quite a few children would eventually end up like this.

No child should ever have to face their own mortality and yet we were learning that, for some, it is exactly what is thrown at them. Life stinks sometimes. Pure and simple, like some great big farmyard manure heap. While one can always leave the farmyard, it is impossible to walk away from your life. And we were finding life extremely pongy by this time!

Diabetes was ruling our lives and it was horrid. Before diabetes, everything now seemed to be in either of two categories, "before" or "after" diabetes; as I have already said, we had been ever so slightly bohemian in our approach to everything, and one of those things was meal times. Now Cole had to eat at certain times, (with only 10 – 15 minutes of leeway either side, if that) six times a day and it was killing us! Food became almost a four letter word in our house, and everyone hated using it, avoiding it like the plague.

One weekend, Nicky had taken Cole with him to work and been late home for dinner by almost an hour; by the time he arrived home, I was simmering with fury whilst at the same time being sick with anxiety and could not even talk to Nicky for fear that I would lose the plot altogether. Then Nicky had said, "I just wanted to give him a break from diabetes; that is why I let him eat fudge and help me for longer instead of having to come home."

I could not believe what I was hearing. Did he not think that I would like to give him a "break" too? Did he not realise that his "break" meant that I would have to be the monster again, as I would now have to get Cole to check his bloods several times over the coming hours as I had no idea how he would respond to fudge, but seriously suspected that it would involve extra injections of insulin? Apparently he did not. Though I now know that he just could not handle the whole situation, at the time, I thought I would cheerfully kill him if given the opportunity.

On another occasion, Nicky had called me from work to say that he was on his way home with a bad cut on his forehead. He arrived in with blood gushing from a cut about an inch and a half long, which ran from just under his hair line in the centre of his forehead towards the outside corner of his left eye. It was about a centimetre in width and missing the flap of skin.

"Hmm, a pencil would sit nicely in that," I commented. "It looks like the pencil groove on a desk."

Having cleaned the cut I told Nicky that it did indeed need stitches and that he had two options. As it was dinner time, and time for Cole to give himself insulin and eat, I was not in the position to take him to the hospital, so if he wished to get it stitched by a doctor he would have to wait an hour or so until dinner was over. The second option was that I could stitch it with steri-strips, (thin bits of plaster that can be crisscrossed over a wound pulling it together), and that I felt confident that this would do amply. After all, he already had many other scars and what would one more matter? He chose the latter, though I am sure he felt very unloved, something I could do nothing about. I had no option but to feed Cole, and I was so tired I had no energy left for sympathy. I knew he was not mortally wounded: physically he would survive; mentally he was on his own. I have to say, that with my "stitching," bathing and with homeopathic remedies, the wound healed beautifully and can now only be seen on extremely close examination!

However, all this "strictness" was putting a terrible strain on both the family and Nicky and myself, so I started to look for alternative ways of insulin management. I found that there were different insulin regimes, and that the one Cole was on was the most basic one. There was another one called MDI (multiple daily injections). With MDI, one slow acting insulin injection is given once a day which slowly releases insulin in minute amounts over 24 hours and aims to mimic your pancreas, which does this normally. Then an injection of rapid-acting insulin is given every time you eat, again mimicking the body's response to when food/glucose enters the system. Immediately one thing screamed out at me. If Cole was on MDI, yes he would have to give more injections, but he would not have to eat as much food, and we would not be forced to eat at specific times! Also, from all that I was reading, it appeared that on MDI one could obtain better control over the dreaded blood glucose (BG)! I rang the hospital and said that I wished Cole to be put on MDI. Oddly, they were not as enthusiastic as I was, and although you would have thought that I would have expected it by now, I did not, and was amazed at how I had to present my case and win them over. I explained that, a) I wished to have better control over Cole's BG levels and, b) that having to eat at strict times was adding a whole lot of stress to the family and making our already tenuous hold on family life even shakier.

After some persuasion, the hospital did give in and changed Cole to MDI and for a short while things improved a little. We got back our bohemian eating regime, though Cole still had to get up by a certain time each day, weekends and holidays included, so that he could give himself the slow acting insulin (basal), as it had to be given at the same time each day without fail or deviation.

However, after about a month, just when we were thinking that maybe we could just about cope with this, God – the creep – decided that we were getting a little too comfortable, and Cole started to feel nauseous. The nausea built up insidiously without us really seeing it. Sounds odd but it was true. Suddenly I realised that Cole was complaining of feeling sick most days. He did not actually get sick in the beginning, but looked ghastly. The sickness built in intensity until he was actually feeling nauseous the whole day long. His face was constantly white with a yellow rim around the hairline. I told the doctors at the hospital but they were not concerned, and said that it was probably a bug. I pointed out that this "bug" was lasting a long time, a month or more, and that from just feeling sick the odd time during the day, he was now nauseous constantly. They shrugged and moved on. I took him to our GP who listened to me and tried different medications, all to no avail.

The nausea, which I can only liken to constant pregnancy morning sickness, was to last two years, during which time I watched my child become more and more despondent and lose the will to live. One of the worst memories I have is of Christmas Day 2007, when Cole was 10. We were all staying with my parents and the children had all just opened their presents. Instead of being able to run around with his sisters and being excited with his new toys from Santa, Cole had climbed back into bed looking and feeling like death warmed up. I climbed in with him and held him close, unable to make him better, my heart breaking for this sick little child who could not even play with his toys.

It occurred to me, on more than one occasion that we as a family had no sooner sorted out one challenge than another one popped up, a bit like some continuous survival game. I had long ago realised that I could not survive if I called things "problems", which to me meant that they were potentially harmful and difficult to overcome, requiring a constant fight or struggle to do so. However, if I looked at each new situation as a "challenge", then I could convince myself that it was just a matter of applying my mental ability to solve it. Of course, I did have days where it was hard to get out of bed and face the day ahead but I could usually pull myself out of my lake of self-pity and get on with the day, even if I was still dripping a little bit for the beginning of it.

The hospital said that they had never seen a case like Cole's. They did not know why he was continuously sick, and once they had run several tests including stools and blood, they were at a loss. When I said that I felt it was linked to the long term (basal) insulin injection - as I had noticed that he appeared to be feeling even more sick shortly after giving it - I was met by that "patient" smile that I had come to recognise so well during my years of reaching out to professionals looking for help for Ariana. I knew what it meant and I hated it. It meant that they were thinking, "I am the professional, you are just the mother. What could you possibly know that I do not? Nothing."

And with that smile, they dismissed me. I tested my theory by changing the time that Cole gave his basal insulin. This was more than a little scary to do on my own because it meant that at a certain point during the changeover Cole would have either too much or too little insulin is his system, depending on how I did things. So, even less sleep for me and more finger pricking for him, as I needed to monitor his blood glucose levels very closely. But I needed to check out my theory, so we changed it from the morning to the evening and yes, he was still definitely feeling sicker just after giving it. I then rang the drug company that produced the particular brand of insulin that Cole was using and asked them had they ever heard of basal insulin causing the user to be nauseous? They said that they had not, and also that they were not at liberty to discuss their drugs with me! I could only talk to a doctor about the drug. I could get no information from them as it would be seen as them promoting their drug and this was not allowed in Ireland. So I went to a pharmacy and asked them if there were other brands of basal insulin? Yes there were. There were older brands that were called human insulin (though they were not actually harvested from humans and were synthetic) and what Cole was on was called analogue insulin, which was a newer and slightly altered form of human insulin. So back I went to the hospital and told them what I had done with the basal insulin, that I felt that it could be the cause of Cole's nausea, and that I wished to look into it. I realised that he needed basal insulin, and I wished to try the human insulin instead of the analogue to see if it made a difference. To say that they were less than pleased with me questioning them or changing Cole's regime without their input, would be an understatement. They agreed to change his insulin, but stated that it would not make any difference as human insulin was the same as analogue insulin. I pointed out that it could not, logically be the same, as the amino acid sequences had been altered in the analogue insulin to change the rate at which it was absorbed from the injection site. They maintained that that was not relevant! I left disillusioned that they could possibly make such a statement. Did they really think that I was that dumb? Which made me angry. Or more frighteningly, did they really believe what they were telling me? How could they? The two insulins were very different structurally; how could they possibly react in the same way? That is like saying a Ferrari is the same as a Fiat because they are both cars! Sure, they both drive from A to B, but one is a hell of a different ride than the other! By now I was aware that the staff at the hospital were just a tad "frosty" towards me.

Cole started to use the older insulin and his nausea did lessen by a considerable amount. While he no longer looked like death warmed up, and as if he was permanently trying to hold down the contents of his stomach, he still felt nauseous all the time.

Then our GP asked us if we had ever considered an insulin pump? He had just seen one and felt that it was definitely worth looking in to. So back I went to the internet, and after looking into it and contacting not only producers but also users, I realised that this might indeed be the answer as insulin pumps only use rapid-acting insulin - no need for the slow-releasing long term insulin which I suspected was the cause of Cole's nausea.

Back to the hospital again with my new information and a request to try putting Cole on an insulin pump. Now the reception went from "frosty" to positively "frozen". They did not "like" insulin pumps. I pointed out, that as a mother, I could not sit back and watch my child slowly lose the will to live. That in the last two years he had effectively missed a year's schooling due to being too sick to either go in the first place, or being so sick on arrival that he had to come straight back home. I told them I could not count the number of mornings that he had bravely climbed into the car feeling nauseous, but after the drive there being so sick that he could not possibly get out of the car; that he was now saying that he no longer wished to live like this and that I was very afraid that he would soon give up on life altogether; that I was not going to sit around and let that happen. I said that I wished to put Cole on an insulin pump to see if he would improve with only rapid insulin. The doctor that I was talking with said, "In my view, to have an insulin pump attached to a child permanently would be abuse."

This is the second time in my life when I have been afraid that social services would be called and my children taken away from me.

As the hospital that we attended did not support insulin pumps, they could not have given him one anyway. But they could have referred him to another hospital that did and they would not.

I went home and rang two hospitals on the east coast that did support insulin pumps and explained Cole's situation. They felt that an insulin pump could help but that I would need to get a referral.

"Does it have to be from his current hospital, or can it be from his GP?" I asked.

"Either."

So back I went to the GP who not only gave us a referral, but also smoothed things over with the hospital by promising them that I would not ask them for any help or support with the pump. More importantly, this letter from one of their own profession supporting me made me a little less afraid that they would set social services on me because I was going against their advice. As I had already learnt in all systems, be it health, teaching or whatever, you have those who genuinely care more about the individual person than the system or what their peers think, and those who are just part of the system and cannot or will not step outside of it. We were lucky in that our GP genuinely cared about Cole. We went to the pump hospital.

# Chapter 12

Going up to the hospital with Cole for his first appointment, I was positively bursting with expectancy and hope. This hospital was putting children on insulin pumps, therefore they must be progressive in their approach and so would be only too willing to help a little boy who was so obviously sick. Because we had health insurance, I went privately to that first appointment as my experience in Ireland had always been that "you got what you paid for". I was so wrong on both of these assumptions.

We met the consultant and were given a 15 minute consultation during which he did not talk with Cole. He asked me a few questions about why I wanted to put Cole on an insulin pump and then said, "You cannot go privately, there is only a public system for this and there is a waiting list" in a bored voice.

The rage that now lived in me just below the surface, and was so quick to try to break free, erupted and I thought I would leap across the table and strangle him. Fighting desperately to stay in control of my feelings, because I also, desperately, wanted that pump to save my child's life, I took a deep breath. I enquired quietly, "Well, can we get on to the waiting list? I was not told that when I made the appointment."

To which he just shrugged his shoulders and said, "Well, that is the way it is. You will have to come back through the public system."

Needing to get on that waiting list, I said nothing more about it and forked out the 120 euro that was his fee for 15 minutes of nothing. He said that an appointment would be sent out to us and we left.

Over the years there have been many times that I have been totally frustrated and furious with the medical care system and those who operated within it. This was one of them and I fought hard not to give in to the urge to scream, rage and cry once we got into the car because I did not want to scare the living daylights out of Cole.

I would like to explain here that I do not swear in real life and find it hard to do so while writing, it just is not me. I have to admit though, that often the expletives would be much more satisfying to utter, and I have been known to do so on two or so occasions. The first was just after Cole went on to the MDI insulin regime. We had stayed the weekend with my parents in Dublin and Cole and I were returning home on Sunday night. After driving for two hours we stopped and bought a take away to eat for tea. We parked, went to check Cole's bloods and give him an injection of insulin only to discover that we had left his "bloods bag", with all his medical gear in it, in Dublin. We both paled and looked at each other. Immediately, Cole started to apologize, something that he had started to do a heart-breaking amount after being diagnosed, as if everything was now somehow his fault. We both knew what this meant: we could not eat, we would not know if he felt "funny" if he was low, and if so, how low? We were afraid, again. I could not help myself; I sat there saying nothing for a moment, as the only word that was screaming in my mind was "FUCK" and I did not want to say it. But I realised that saying nothing was worse, as Cole might think I was cross with him, so I opened my mouth and said it. Having said it once, I could not stop. It was as if a dam, that had been holding back all I felt about the rubbish that had happened to us over the last few years, had just broken, and I repeated the word about ten times, with distinction and clarity, and then burst into tears. Cole was so shocked that he stopped apologizing, so that was good! After we had both hugged each other, each trying to reassure the other that everything was going to be alright, we both shakily laughed at my odd outburst, and the fact that I had being pronouncing the word as if I was in an elocution lesson. Then Cole nobly said, "Mum, you eat. I don't mind. I will wait till we get home."

"Cole, if you do not get to eat, then I am not eating either. But I thank you. We will both eat together when we get home, if we are still hungry in another two hours."

From that day on, we left spares in the car, though even this is not fool proof because insulin only survives out of the fridge for a month. Invariably we sometimes forget to change it; and while the makers of blood glucose meters are adamant that their meters should not be left in cars as they do not like extremes of temperature, we run that risk as better a chance that it will work than not having the chance at all.

We waited for the pump appointment and kept it when it came, but now I was not so positive about the hospital or its staff being either progressive or caring anymore. When we got to the appointment, it was the same consultant that we had seen before but now just wearing his "public system" hat. Again, he hardly acknowledged Cole's existence, only doing so to tell him to drop his trousers to show him his injection sites on his legs. Cole was mortified and obviously did not want to do it, so I asked could he not feel the sites through his trousers as the previous doctors had?

"No, if he will not show me, we cannot do anymore."

Cole was 10 years old. The doctor never spoke to him, never reassured him, and never created any rapport with him at all. And I was the one who had subtly been accused of abuse?

During the appointment I had explained Cole's whole medical history since his diagnosis of diabetes. I may as well have saved my breath.

"We will start by putting Cole back on mixed insulin and observe what happens from there."

What I said was, "I do not want him to go back on to mixed insulin. We have done that, and I have told you all that has happened since then. Cole has just one and a half years until he starts secondary school, he has missed a huge amount of school already and if this is not sorted out he will be way behind and unable to catch up." And I spoke quietly.

What I really wanted to YELL at him was, "Have you not been listening to anything I said? Over my dead body are we going back to the beginning again. I think you are a completely unsympathetic sod, and were you even taught how to interact with patients?"

But of course I did not, as I was completely at his mercy; he was the one who decided to whom a pump was given.

In all we had three appointments with this consultant over a course of six months. At the first appointment I asked what the criteria was for being put on a pump. He said good control - good blood glucose readings and HbA1c readings. HbA1c readings are a blood glucose reading that the hospital can do that shows what your average blood glucose reading has been for the previous three months. It is informative to know because it shows how you are managing overall, balancing out the "high" and "low" readings. So from that appointment I had been on a mission. We succeeded in having excellent blood glucose readings most of the time, and Cole's HbA1c came down constantly, from in the 11%s that he had at diagnosis, to in the 9%s and wavered around there. In an ideal world you would like the HbA1c to be somewhere between 5.5% and 7.5%, but that is tight, tight control.

I was handicapped in what I could do. To obtain optimum control one needs to be able to give the correct amount of insulin for the amount of carbohydrates in the food one eats. To be able to do this one needs to know, 1) which foods contain carbohydrates, 2) how many carbohydrates they contain and, 3) how many carbohydrates one unit of insulin covers. This is called carbohydrate (or carb) counting, and when Cole was put onto MDI I asked the hospital how I could learn about this. Was there a course for parents of children with type 1 diabetes? By now you will probably not be very surprised to learn that no, there is no course available in Ireland for parents to learn this. So parents are left to "guess" the amount of carbohydrates that are in each food, while the amount of carbohydrates each unit of insulin covers for their child is estimated by the medical professionals based on the weight of the child. As you have probably realised, guessing does not lead to stable blood glucose readings. Parents can give too much insulin sometimes and too little at others. Also, as different foods release their carbohydrates at different rates, and exercise means that your metabolism uses insulin more efficiently, one unit of insulin covers more carbohydrates when your child is active than when your child is inactive. So basically, at best, you haven't got a hope in hell of getting it right enough of the time; at worst, it is complete negligence on the part of the medical system, as many children and adults experience far more lows and highs than they need too.

So even with this handicap, we did really well in controlling Cole's blood glucose levels and lowering his HbA1c, but it was excruciating. It meant that I was adapting, learning and managing his diabetes, day and night, every day and night, full time. No time out, no breaks, no holidays. So when we went back for the second appointment three months later and the consultant turned around and told me that, "We have changed our criteria for putting children on pumps. We are now giving them to children with poor blood glucose control", I think a jury may have acquitted me if I had murdered him then and there. I didn't. I just sat completely shell shocked for a few moments and then said, "I have done everything that you told me to do since we were here last, and it has been extremely difficult to achieve, and now you are telling me that Cole is even further down the waiting list than before?"

"Yes, but you have done very well."

"Yes, but how long till Cole will get a pump?"

"Oh, I could not say. Maybe six months, maybe a year."

I said that I thought they were being very unfair changing their criteria like that, especially when we had striven so hard to meet it. They grew frosty and said that surely I would not like to see some child who was sick and unwell have to wait for a pump when my child was doing so well? I pointed out that my child was sick and unwell all the time. They said, ah yes, but his blood glucose and HbA1c readings are excellent. It did not matter what I said, they would not move Cole up the waiting list as he no longer met their criteria. End of appointment; no more discussion; come back in three months and we will see how he is doing.

Now I am a loving person, some people even think that I am too loving, but I can tell you that at this point in time there raged inside of me a hatred so strong that it frightened me. It threatened to consume me and all I could think of was of all those whom I perceived as having so grievously mistreated me and my family over the last few years. It was a very dark time and took me a while to come out of it. I did not enjoy it. I did not like hating. I knew that I had to find a way of letting go of it or I would become ill. I have now found my way back and several things have helped along the way. One of them, strange as it may seem, was getting a tattoo - much to my mother's horror, as nice girls do not have tattoos. But to me it is a symbol of what I know to be true, that I can change my life, no matter what. It is a beautiful red and orange line drawing of a phoenix and it is on the inside of my forearm where I can see it first thing when I wake up, so that no matter how hard things may seem that morning or how stinky life is, I know I can rise above it and change my life to what I want it to be. A phoenix never dies; it is continually reborn out of the ashes and rises back up to soar wherever it wishes, to greatness. Also phoenix tears are healing. It has always seemed to me a sign that all will be alright, eventually, that I had given Cole, Phoenix as a middle name when he was born, and way back before any of this had ever happened.

My tattoo has kept me going through many a challenging time and it has been healing. Yoga has also played an important role in my life, and I try to practise it every day, even if it is just for 15 minutes, though longer helps me more. I find it calming and it helps me to keep a positive outlook on life. And homeopathy has really helped me stay sane; it has helped me deal with my grief, my rage and my despondency, along with many physical ailments that have come up for me along the way. Everything is a work in progress; as life evolves, so do I with the tools that I have found along the way to help me.

When Cole and I went back in three months' time, I asked Nicky to come with us. I wanted his view, to make sure that I was not in any way reacting as an irrational mother, which is what the medical profession by and large have always maintained. When we went into the appointment, the consultant welcomed Nicky in the spirit of bonhomie, of one male meeting another, and afforded him a respect that I had never received. He also had the head DSN (diabetes specialist nurse) come and sit in on the appointment, again something that had never happened before. During the whole appointment, both of them addressed everything to Nicky, even though Nicky constantly said, "Kelly is the primary caregiver", "Kelly finds this" and, "Kelly has seen this." Never once did he put himself in the primary position; it was always me, and yet they never once spoke to me. Nor did they say anything to Cole. Worse, when we left the appointment Cole was no nearer to getting the pump and they still could not give us a date.

Once back in the car I asked Nicky, "So what do you think? How do you feel?"

He thought for a while and then said, "Shafted." And then he swore a bit more for good measure. As you can see, he has no trouble with language!

That about summed it up. We were getting nowhere, and we were being treated abominably.

# Chapter 13

We came home from the meeting feeling angry and disillusioned again, and wondering how to get off of this merry-go-round. It is all too easy, when the going is tough, to wallow in self-pity. I know this as I have been there, but I also know that it does not achieve anything. For me the only way to survive was to cut contact with anyone who was not positive. This may sound callous, but I was already dealing with so much negativity from those I was now forced into contact with regarding Cole and Ariana's health needs, that I could not take anymore. What I needed from my friends was that when I moaned about something challenging, that they just listened but did not commiserate, and definitely did not say, "Oh, poor you, I have absolutely no idea how you manage," because I sure as hell did not either, but had to believe that I could; that if I cried one day and was cheerful the next, that they took it at face value and realised that, yes, I was putting a brave face on things and to just let me; and not to ask me about the rubbish that was going on in our lives.

Ariana was at least able to attend school and socialise with the children there, even if it totally wiped her out and we then had to spend hours each evening interpreting what had happened in school each day. She was, most of the time, going in on her own due to Cole being so ill, something I would not have dreamt possible only months earlier. Thea was happy at boarding school, though desperately hurting when home because I could not give her any undivided attention, no time for just her and me, as I was always helping Ariana or Cole. And Cole was dying before my eyes. He was becoming weaker and weaker emotionally the longer the sickness continued. He was giving up the will to live; it was just too hard for him.

So I went back to the drawing board, or in this case, the internet. I searched for groups who were insulin pump users and found one in England. I sent them an email briefly outlining our problem and asking them if they knew of anywhere in England that we could attend privately to get an insulin pump. They replied that indeed they did, and gave me the information, but they also stated that under the NICE guidelines, they thought my child was entitled to get an insulin pump in Ireland. Actually, the NICE (National Institute for Clinical Excellence) guidelines cover England and Northern Ireland but not the Republic of Ireland, and while I was pretty sure that there would be a European equivalent covering Ireland, and I did think about fighting the system for a pump for Cole, that could have taken years, and it definitely would have had an extremely detrimental effect on my health and our family. So I called the clinic in England and spoke with the DSN (diabetes specialist nurse) whose name I had been given. She was the loveliest of ladies, and it was the first time that I felt heard and afforded any respect. She also had a child, who was now an adult, who had type 1 diabetes, so she could totally relate to my fears and anguishes. Right from the start, this lady made a remarkable difference in our lives. She told me that yes, it was possible to put Cole on an insulin pump, and that she totally agreed with me that it was the right thing to try. When would we like to come over? As simple as that. Except not. The pump itself would cost us approximately €5,500, and then there were the other costs. I would need to fly over to London for one day a week, for three weeks, to attend a carbohydrate and insulin dose adjustment course. Then, on week four, Cole and I would need to fly to London and spend a week there, attending the clinic each day to be shown how the insulin pump worked and for him to be set up on it and monitored. I figured that, all in all, it could cost us anywhere up to €15,000. Money that we just did not have. So Nicky and I decided that we would just have to put it on our credit card and hope that the money came from somewhere, as the other option – to do nothing, while waiting for the healthcare system to maybe help us, and just watch Cole die – was not an option at all.

Even before Cole got the pump, life became easier as I learnt how to count carbohydrates and to work out the amount of insulin that he needed for them. His blood glucose readings stopped swinging so violently between the "highs" and "lows" and were far more stable. While it was not a doddle, neither was it rocket science.

Within 12 hours of Cole being connected to the insulin pump and only receiving rapid insulin, his nausea went! After two years of being told that it could not possibly be related to the basal insulin, I could see that it was, without a shadow of a doubt, exactly that. We removed the basal insulin and the nausea stopped - that simple. Cole and I were euphoric. We spent the week in London learning how to use the pump and the continuous glucose monitor (CGM) that communicated with the pump. I began to realise just how amazing this piece of technology was. I learnt how to run tests to check that the settings for Cole's basal/background insulin were correct. I could work out and programme in information into the pump, so that when Cole wanted to eat, all he had to do was to enter in his blood glucose reading and the pump's "wizard" would do all the calculations for him. I told the pump what Cole's blood glucose levels should be during the day and the night, which meant that if the CGM told the pump that Cole's bloods were below a certain level, the pump suspended all insulin delivery until he was above this level and alarmed to alert Cole to the fact that he was going low. If his blood glucose levels were "high", it would alarm and, with a few presses of a button, tell Cole how much insulin was needed to correct the "high". If they were "low", but not at suspend level, and Cole wished to eat, it would work out by how much Cole's insulin needed to be reduced to stay within safe levels. It had several ways in which to deliver insulin to match the type of food Cole was eating. So for instance, if he wanted to eat or drink something that released its sugar rapidly, say sweets, Cole could give the insulin up front. However, if he wished to eat something that released its sugar slowly, such as a fatty food like chips, he could tell the pump to give him some insulin up front and some on a time delay. And all this was just the tip of the iceberg!

Cole came home from London a different child. Over the next month, the independent and naturally inquisitive child that we had lost, began to return. I can safely say that it took me six months to become confident that I was not going to make a hash of it every time I touched the pump. I checked, rechecked and rechecked all my calculations, as I was terrified that I would input information that would allow Cole to overdose on insulin. It required constant and dedicated work but without a shadow of a doubt it was so worth it. And I always had the backup of the nurse in London; I even had her home number for emergencies, though I never used it. That pump gave Cole back his independence and his chance of having a "normal" life. It is Cole's pancreas, which now just happens to live on the outside of his body.

A month after we returned from getting the pump, Cole had a check-up appointment in our local hospital. We went in to it feeling extremely nervous and a bit like we were walking towards a meeting with the hangman. The last time we had been there we had left in tears. We had asked to try out a CGM to see if it could shed any light on Cole's nausea, and after waiting several months the opportunity had arisen just before we went to London. As we were already off the "nice list" in the hospital and firmly on the "naughty list", I had not wanted to seem ungrateful when they offered us this opportunity, and so we had gone in to get it fitted and try it out. When we met the nurse we were rather taken aback by her somewhat glacial attitude, as she had always been so nice and kind before, and I could only suppose that it was because she too felt aggrieved that I wished to put Cole on an insulin pump. However, I was horrified that she let this show in her manner towards Cole. The CGM had to be inserted by a spring loaded device at an angle of 45 degrees to the abdomen, and the needle that it was delivering was about an inch long and by no means thin. Cole was terrified of it. He tried really hard to stand there and let her near him with it, but always at the last minute his courage failed him and he shied away. I asked her if I could be the one to do it.

"No. These cost €60 each", she replied, as if the cost meant that only paid representatives of the hospital were able to handle such a valuable commodity.

"Well, I will pay for it then because I know that Cole would rather I did it," I replied.

"No, that is not possible."

I tried to calm Cole and to talk him into letting her do it, but try as he might he could not and the waves of disapproval that emanated from her did not help. After 20 minutes or so she said, "Well, this has been a waste of time."

I could not believe it! Cole visibly shrank before my eyes into a sad and despondent heap. I wanted to slap her and demand how she could treat a child this way, but I knew that we would have to come back to the hospital and that we were, once again, at the system's mercy.

"Well, I do not think so. Come on, Cole, let's go to the toy shop. I think that for being so very brave and trying so hard you deserve a treat." And with that, I swept both of us out of her office without a word of farewell or a backward glance.

My bravado lasted until the carpark, and once in the car, both Cole and I, burst into tears while clinging to each other. Over and over, Cole kept saying how sorry he was that he could not do it.

"Cole, I am so proud of you for trying. It was a huge device and needle. I was scared of it. I think that the nurse behaved incredibly badly. I don't know why, but probably because we are going to get a pump. But I also bet you anything that she has never put one of them into herself, so she has no idea how scary it is."

So that had been our last visit to the hospital, and while we were now able to insert CGM's - due to the wonderful nurse in London, who had given Cole an anaesthetic cream to put on the insertion site, who had spent over an hour with me encouraging Cole to do the first one and who had allowed me to be the one to insert it – we were both terrified of what our reception would be like.

When it was Cole's turn to be seen, we were given a trainee doctor so I knew right from the start that we had been written off. Before this, we had been seen by one of the long term staff, maybe with a trainee in tow, but never cut loose on their own. Well, that was fine with me! All I needed was for them to monitor his weight, height and HbA1c to make sure that he was within the limits for his age. At the moment the one that concerned me most was his height, as in the last two years since he had been sick he had stopped growing at the same rate as before. Previously, he had always been one of the taller children for his age, whereas now he was only just about average, maybe even tending towards below average.

The trainee asked us how Cole was getting on, so I proceeded to tell him how wonderful the pump was and how Cole was no longer sick and that life was so much easier for him. I even produced some charts that I had printed off from the information that I was able to download from the pump. He became very excited and said, "And Cole's HbA1c has dropped down to the 7's! This is wonderful. I must tell the professor!"

And before I knew what was happening he had shot out of the room. I did not share his optimism and was not so sure how the professor would react, as he had been less than enthusiastic before. So I turned to Cole and said, "Cole, when the professor comes in, I want you to answer all his questions. We know that the pump is wonderful, but now we must sell it to him. If there is ever any hope of any other children being given the opportunity to have a pump from this hospital, it is up to us to show them how great it is."

When the professor came in he started to ask Cole questions straight away, ignoring me, as I had thought would happen. Cole was brilliant and answered everything with detail. Then the professor turned to me and it was my turn. After I had answered his questions, he put his hands up in the position of surrender and said, "Hands up. You were right and I was wrong."

I completely choked up. Never in a million years had I expected that. Here was my opportunity to read him the riot act - to say how hard he and his team had made it for me to help Cole, how much needless misery Cole had gone through - but I didn't. I have never seen the point in castigating someone when they are being big enough to admit the error of their ways or when they are down. I have always believed that we all learn far faster and far more from those who are kind, patient and loving with us, so instead of making him squirm, I offered our help. "If you would like to know anything more about the pump, Cole and I would be more than happy to answer any questions. Especially if it meant that it would help another child."

He thanked me and went on his way and we left to go home. I was walking on air. Sure, every day we would still have to manage Cole's diabetes, that was a given, and most days life seemed to throw us a curve ball; we could never, ever take anything for granted, but now we had a wonderful piece of technology to help us, and I no longer had to fight the hospital. While they may not have been my best buddies, they were no longer bordering on being my enemies and that was huge.

So this is how our relationship has remained over the years - tentative and wary. I do not take anything they say as gospel without first researching it. I wish to be in control with them there to help should we ever be in the need of it. They allow this as they had nothing to do with the setup of Cole's pump, but it is an alien arrangement for them, and we are an oddity. I feel I am more knowledgeable of Cole's diabetes as I eat, live, breathe, sleep with Cole's (and his sisters') welfare foremost in my consciousness. A different doctor sees him once every four months for fifteen minutes, during which time he is personally in their consciousness; then we leave and he is out of their consciousness, and they move on. I know exactly how Cole's diabetes affects him; how his blood sugar levels are likely to respond to any given situation we have met. They know what they have learnt in college and clinically along the way. They have never "lived" with diabetes, and constantly, every day forever, monitored themselves or their child in order to keep them alive, with the knowledge that if they get it wrong, death is dancing on his toes just around the corner, ever waiting. You see, I am beyond highly motivated; they are at best motivated. To them it is a job, to me it means life. So I think my desire to be in control, with them in the background, is an entirely reasonable and logical one. And my supreme goal, the one to which I am constantly teaching, working, promoting and cajoling, is that Cole will be in control. His safe independence is my ultimate aim.

# Chapter 14

Now you may think that we had a lovely break here, that life sailed along pleasantly for a while, because surely now we had had our fair share of life's trials and tribulations; but what no one understands, unless they have a child with a permanent health challenge, is that there are no breaks, not ever.

A wonderful thing did happen though. A distant, elderly relative of Nicky's, whom we did not know, died and left us (well him, but what's his is mine and vice versa, though sometimes I think he wonders how love equates in monetary terms; I, of course, assure him that it is far more valuable) some money. Yay! You may think that I am completely heartless to say that this was a wonderful thing, but it was and we were so thankful to them! It meant that we were able to pay for the insulin pump and all the costs involved with getting it. It also meant that for a while we knew where the money was coming from to pay the school fees for Théa (and Ariana who was about to start), and we could also pay off the previous loan taken out for that purpose. It gave us a year or two's breathing space, financially. This was huge, as there is a massive financial burden that comes with any child's health challenge, which people outside of the family do not see, and it is not one that any health insurance or government covers. Parents of children with challenges spend all their available – and a lot of the time, unavailable – money on trying to find ways to help that child. It is not possible for us to wait on a list on the public healthcare system, as it can take months to get an appointment. We cannot afford to wait at all because our child is deteriorating before our eyes, slipping further and further away from us, beyond our reach into a world of their own, or towards death because they cannot bear to be in this world anymore; it is just too painful.

For these children, the possibility of choosing death over life is a very real possibility, and yet one that is rarely, if ever, talked about. The rates of suicides for children on the autistic spectrum is higher than average, (Dickerson, 2013) as it also is for children with other challenges such as type1 diabetes. Yet it is not looked at or addressed - probably because it makes adults feel uncomfortable to acknowledge that maybe we are part of a system/belief that can fail a child so badly that they would rather choose death than life. And what of those whom we trust to help us, such as the medical profession or the government? Well, it seems to me that those in power rarely admit their shortcomings or failings. Perhaps they feel we would be disillusioned with them? Perhaps they are afraid that if they admit they are only human, like the rest of us, that we would start to think for ourselves and look for our own solutions? Whatever the reason, not admitting to, and not addressing, the problem is not the solution.

So I researched every alternative that I could find, either online or that I heard of by word of mouth. Over the years I researched many different modalities: acupuncture, allopathic medicine (mainstream medicine), chelation, craniosacral massage, detoxing, diet (GAP, whole30), EFT (emotional freedom technique), healers (those who had healed themselves of illness, such as Byron Katie), homeopathy, Reiki - to name but a few. When I had researched them in depth with a view to either helping the children with autism or type1 diabetes or boosting their immune system, I tried out those that I felt had something to offer. Strangely, by doing this, by being a committed and proactive mum who was dedicated to improving my children's quality of life, I came up against ridicule and derision. I discovered that most of the people I knew were skeptics, and that they were not afraid of voicing their opinions, even though I never asked for them. Their opinion seemed to be that any modality that was not allopathic (conventional medicine) was hogwash and quackery, and that anyone who tried them was a fool and of diminished intelligence.

The really odd thing was that when I asked them if they had any first-hand experience of the modality they were writing off, they said no; when I then asked them on what they were basing their opinion on, they said, "science"; when I asked them to show me this "science" they could not; but they still were adamant that I was a fool. I could explain why I was trying out the modality in question; I could show them my research into that modality; I could back up my reasoning and they could not, but I was the fool? They said that I was wasting my money and my time; that I was throwing Nicky's and my savings down the drain. When I asked them what they would have me do to help our children, they looked blankly at me or told me to go to the doctor. I told them that I had been to the doctor, in fact, to many doctors and no one was offering me any ways in which to help my children. They then said how sad it was that there was no known way to help my children lead normal lives, and would I not just try to be happy and grateful with what we had in life, and save our money for when we needed it, like when the children wanted to go to university or Nicky retired? I tried, I really did, to explain to these people that I could not just sit back and do nothing, that one of our children was under such duress and stress trying to deal with every day social interactions that she was wondering if it might not be easier to die, and that another of our children had been so sick 24 hours a day, seven days a week for two years that he too had said that he was not sure that he could keep trying to live; that to be planning for university seemed just a tad irrelevant considering that two of my children might not even live that long. They could not hear this; they would shift from foot to foot or squirm in their chairs and then, because they were so uncomfortable with the thought that children could commit suicide, they would say that I was overreacting!

Many had never even been in my house, and even if they had, they had never lived with us for a few days and experienced our lives. Yet they felt happy to tell me that I was overreacting and wrong because it made them feel better. However, what really got to me about all this, is that they were happy to take away my hope. They were telling me that I was to just accept that my children were suffering. In fact, they would not believe that they were suffering, and that I should actually be grateful and do nothing because they, along with a lot of doctors, believed that MD meant medical deity and not medical doctor, and that if the medical profession had said there was nothing to be done, then there was no point in even trying! It did not matter that they all admitted, on questioning, that none of the modalities that I was exploring did any harm; I should just not try them. These people were happy to ridicule and dismiss that which they did not know and had not tried out, to try to impose their will and opinions, which were based solely on hearsay, on me, and by so doing strip me of that which keeps us all going - hope and belief. To me that was, and still is, one of the cruellest things that one human being can do to another.

So while Cole was healthy again and only needed my help constantly with managing his blood glucose levels, Ariana was now struggling. She had finished her primary schooling, and sadly there was no Steiner secondary school for her to go onto to finish her education. So we looked around at all the possibilities and talked them over with her. In the end, she decided that she would have the best chance in the lovely Quaker run boarding school that her older sister was now attending, loving and thriving in. She did not really want to leave me or home where she felt safe and loved no matter how different she was. However, we all felt that the local alternatives were far too similar to the local primary school system that had failed her so badly; hardly a surprising conclusion, as all were state run and followed the same restrictive structure.

For the first year and a half she struggled valiantly through every day. It was incredibly hard for us all. Ariana would call me several times a day (sometimes it could to be up to twenty times), so that I could interpret for her the behaviour of the other children in her year and that of the teachers. In the first year I had the wonderful support of the "matron," a lovely woman who was in charge of the girls' boarding house whom I could ring at any time if I was worried about Ariana, and who offered incredible support to us. These phone calls were stress in themselves for Ariana as she did not want the other children to know that she needed to call me, that she did not understand them, so she would call from the toilets and whisper down the line to me. Inevitably, I could not hear all that she was saying and I would have to ask her to repeat things. This made the conversations longer and would heighten her already agitated state, as she had had to leave class to make the call and she was not supposed to be using her phone during the school day and was afraid of being caught. Her biggest fear was that her phone would be taken from her and that she would lose her connection to me, the only person who could help her to understand this alien world. This fear was so great that we actually got her a second mobile so that we could get rid of at least one fear. Ha! Fat chance, that it would be that easy. Ariana constantly lived in a "what if" world. So the scenario would run like this:

What if her phone got confiscated or she lost it? Well, she now had a backup. But what if that phone too fell down the loo, got lost or confiscated? It did not matter that I would say that I would call the headmaster and that he would get her phone back to her. Because what if he were to say no? It did not matter that I would say that I knew he would not say no, as he was a very caring and genuine man, who I knew from my previous experiences with him, cared deeply about each individual pupil's happiness. But what if he was having a bad day? Because she would point out that I had never had to talk to him in this scenario before, and maybe I had also never talked to him on a bad day, so I could not possibly know, without a shadow of a doubt, that he would react in the way that I predicted. On her part, it was all thought out from a purely logical point of view. My beliefs carried no weight, she had no ability to transpose a solution that had worked in one scenario to another unless the setting and situation was exactly the same - and I mean exactly the same: the same issue, the same room, the same person, wearing the same clothes, smelling of the same perfume/deodorant, having the same facial expression and the same tone of voice - which is never going to happen. On my side, it was constant reassurance, constant interpreting of what she was seeing because she could not read anything. What did a down-turned mouth mean? Was it a sad or cross face? Or was that just their normal face? Why had the person changed their smell? Was it because they wore a different perfume when they were happy or sad? Did the fact that they were wearing red clothes today and black clothes yesterday mean that yesterday they were unhappy and today they were happy? They were speaking quietly when they normally spoke much louder; did this mean they were tired or cross? They were laughing - were they laughing with her or at her? Did they like her or were they making fun of her? And on and on, there was no breaking system because there was no safety net. At home, or with my parents, there was a safety net in that we loved her no matter what; so if she did take a chance in a situation and got it wrong, it did not matter; we would explain what we had meant, make it right and no one would laugh at her only with her, big difference.

You and I take many queues from the person to whom we are talking. We see that their mouth is turned down when normally it is not. At the same time we hear that their voice is quiet when normally it is louder. We notice that their fists are clenched and that their whole body is rigid, and we notice that their eyes are smaller/tighter. Thus we can "feel" they are cold. We know that this person is very angry with us or someone else. Ariana saw these signs but could not read them or put them together. Most heart-breaking was the fact that she could not tell why her peers were laughing. She was always living in a state of anguish and fear that they were laughing at her and not with her, that she was the butt of some joke and looking foolish. My heart broke continually for her. Often she would be in tears, and due to the stress, she started to get symptoms of cystitis most days.

And yet when we had urine samples tested the doctors could find no bacteria present. Sometimes she would become so desperate that she would ring me late at night and say that she just had to leave; she just wanted to walk out of there and come home. It was either that or cause to herself some physical pain, such as stabbing a pen into the palm of her hand until it either really hurt or made it bleed, that would be so great that it over took the mental pain inside of her. Ariana has always spoken the truth. It is impossible for her to lie, so I knew that she would answer my questions truthfully.

"Do you need me to come and get you now, lovey?" It was a three hour drive to her at that time of the night/morning.

"No."

"You will not do anything like leave the school will you?"

"No." Sob.

"Or hurt yourself?" This was my biggest fear, that she would decide that she had had enough of this world, this pain, and leave us permanently.

"No." Sniff.

"Promise."

"Yes, but you will come for me first thing in the morning?"

"Yes, straight after I have left Cole to school. Is that alright?"

"Yes."

And then we would talk for longer, maybe even an hour, me talking about anything and everything that I knew made her happy -

visiting my parents who she loves and who love her just as she is, and who can laugh with her and not take offence when she finds things that they do funny and quirky; all of us doing things as a family, such as being on holiday and swimming which she adores; movies that we had seen and loved; funny things that Cole had said or done that made us laugh - and when I was sure that she would be alright until I reached her later that day, that she would not harm herself or walk out into the city at night on her own, we would hang up and I would snatch a few restless and troubled hours sleep.

Often Ariana would only make it through four days of the school week, and sometimes, if life was proving particularly stressful, Nicky would leave her and Théa back to school on the Sunday night, and I would find myself picking her back up on the Monday. The school were lovely, though. They listened to my explanations of what I thought was happening for Ariana. They believed me. They never put her under any undue stress to preform to a certain standard. They accepted her for herself, and let us do the best we could.

All this was incredibly hard for Théa. She was just 15 years of age by then. When it was time for them to return to school on a Sunday night, Ariana would drag her heels, and in the beginning cry because she did not want to leave me. Théa, who had not felt homesick for a long time, found she was experiencing it again and resented Ariana for it. Then, when they reached school, Ariana was so upset trying to second guess every possible scenario that might arise during the coming week, that all of Nicky's attention would be taken up reassuring her that she would be alright, and that of course I would come and get her if she needed us, and he sometimes forgot to say a proper goodbye to Théa. She was incredibly hurt by this as she has always adored her father and felt incredibly close to him, so she resented Ariana even more. Then, during the week when I was talking with Théa, I would be so anxious for Ariana that I could not help myself and would ask her to please look out for her sister, and she would feel that I only talked to her so that I could ask her to look after her sister, that I did not really care about her or have much interest in what she was doing.

I was very much aware that I was hanging on to one daughter by the skin of my teeth, literally keeping her anchored here in this world, while at the same time I was losing my connection with my other daughter, my first born. Théa felt, and she was right, that she had spent much of her life on the side-lines. Left out and forced to give up her share of me. I was heartbroken that this was how she felt and that it was all true. Théa could make allowances for Cole because he had a "disease" with a name; it was unfair and she could relate to that. Also, Cole is the easiest going of people emotionally; he will fit in anywhere, so he stole none of my time that she felt should have been hers. However, when it came to Ariana, it was a whole different story. All Théa could see was that she stole every single piece of my attention in what she saw as an extremely selfish, self-centred manner. So even though Théa could see that Ariana was in pain and did not want to be like she was, (as she would often say things like, "You all must hate me; I would hate me if I were you" or, "I bet you just wish that you had had another daughter like Théa instead of me" or, "If I was dead all of your lives would be so much better" or, "I wish I didn't act like this; why am I so different to Théa and Cole?"), Théa could not forgive her because there was no name or label of a disease that she could attribute all of Ariana's issues to. My suspicion that Ariana was on the autistic spectrum was not enough. I could not explain why Ariana acted like she did, why she got upset, why she could not understand people, and it certainly did not help that when we were out Ariana would have meltdowns and we would have to leave wherever we were, or else cajole her into continuing to participate in the event at hand, or at least to wait for us while we finished it.

There is one thing that Théa has come to realise though, recently. She has her privacy. She has never had to play her life out in the public arena, being constantly stared at and talked about, as in Ariana's case, or prodded and poked and questioned as in Cole's. So while, as she is quick to point out, she features very little in this book that is how she likes it - private.

Homeopathy helped in that Ariana could take a remedy each time she got the cystitis feelings and they would get better, but nothing was able to stop them reoccurring. And even though I took her to doctors and homeopaths, no one seemed to be able to ease her mental anguish. When Ariana was 14 and in second year, we were again at the doctor's to get a urine sample checked. He suggested that Ariana might benefit from seeing a therapist and gave us the number of one. Today, I cannot remember what kind of therapist she was, but she made a huge difference to our lives by doing nothing. When I called her and explained Ariana's situation she said, "Of course I can see Ariana, but from what you are telling me, I think that what would benefit her most at the moment, would be for her to see a clinical psychologist and be assessed, because I suspect that she is on the autistic spectrum."

I could not believe my ears. After all these years of me saying this to doctors and teachers and not being believed, here was someone who, after listening to me on the phone for ten minutes, was saying the same thing, and not only telling me whom Ariana needed to see, but also recommending someone to me! I thanked her profusely, got off the phone, rang the clinical psychologist and made an appointment.

I liked the clinical psychologist right from the start. He addressed his remarks to both Ariana and me; he listened to us and our reasons for coming to him. Then he explained that he would need to do an assessment, and that to do this he would need to carry out semi-structured clinical interviews with Ariana and me, together and separately, and that a series of screening questionnaires would need to be filled in separately by Ariana and her family in order to get a full understanding of the situation. We readily agreed and, over the course of several months with regular meetings, this took place. In the end we had our diagnosis. Ariana had Asperger's syndrome, which is part of the autistic spectrum. Not only did she meet all the criteria for Asperger's but the psychologist also commented that he found it remarkable that Ariana could attend boarding school at all. In fact, he said that he felt it was totally due to the fact that over the years I had spent so much time helping Ariana to interpret everyday life. He commended my tenacity and dedication as a loving mother. After we left his office for the last time with our diagnosis, his report and his offer of any further help that he could offer in the future, and when I was alone, so as not to upset Ariana, I wept.

I wept for many reasons. I wept that my child had Asperger's in the first place, because life was such a struggle for her and us; but I also wept because finally, after ten long years of being ridiculed and derided, I had been proven correct in my beliefs and actions. For Ariana, the diagnosis in itself brought some comfort in the fact that she now knew that she was not a freak - her sentiment, not mine. There was a reason that she acted and behaved in the way that she did. For me it meant that I now had someone backing me up in a profession that people respected and would listen to, who confirmed what I had been saying for years and which no one would believe. However, it did not bring us any help for her condition. There was no help to be had anywhere unless you went fighting for it, and any help that may have been available was only to offer ways of coping with Asperger's, certainly not to cure it.

So I went back to my computer and started researching again, the psychologist's comments having patched up and fortified my resolve and belief in myself, which had taken a severe bashing over the years. By this stage, it was not possible to research autism without questioning whether vaccinations were linked to it, as there were an abundance of parents all over the world saying the same thing - their child had been developing normally until they had been given a vaccination, and then they had developed autism, (go to you tube and put in "hear this well"). So again I began to ask if vaccines were safe. It also occurred to me to look at the diseases for which vaccines were developed, and of which I, and every other parent, were told to be mortally afraid of, as they would kill or maim our child.

# Chapter 15

Before I started to research diseases for which there were vaccinations, I looked at what I thought I knew, the assumptions I had based my beliefs on.

Assumption number one: vaccines were great because they stopped children getting diseases that were more than likely to kill them or maim them terribly.

Assumption number two: deaths from these diseases had declined solely because of the vaccines.

Assumption number three: vaccines were safe.

I looked at measles first because, to me, that was the obvious one, as every now and again I heard in the media about an outbreak of measles and of a child who died from the disease; and I realised that this subconsciously frightened me every time.

I learnt that measles at the beginning of the 20th century was indeed what could be termed, "a killer" disease. At that time it was responsible for more deaths than diphtheria, smallpox and scarlet fever together. In England, from the turn of the century to after the First World War (1900-1918), an average of 10 to 12 thousand children died every year from measles. However, between 1918 and the 1950s, the number of children dying from measles fell sharply, and by the 1950s there was an average of 100 deaths per year. In 1940 the death rate for measles was one child in every 690 and by 1960 the death rate was one child in every 10,000. All this happened before a vaccine was introduced. Based on this trend from before the vaccine was introduced, the prediction would be that by 2007, less than one child a year would have died from measles. (Halvorsen, 2007)

Also I learnt that measles weakens the immune system, and most often children did not die from measles, but a secondary, opportunistic disease such as pneumonia, and that children whose immunity was poor were more susceptible. Children suffering from malnutrition are at far higher risk, and this was known back in the early 1900s. In 1931, a child in the poorest social class was 20 times more likely to die than a child in in the highest class. (Halvorsen, 2007)

Between 2001 and 2004 there were four reported deaths from measles within 19 European countries and only one was a child. Often the media did not report the full story, as in the case of a 13 year old boy who died from measles in 2006 in England. It was implied that the we needed to be afraid of an outbreak of measles as it had already killed this boy. What was not reported though was that the boy was on immunosuppressive drugs and that these drugs and his underlying condition increased his risk from measles and also any other disease. In 2008 the same was true when a 17- year-old boy died from measles who suffered from immune problems. (Halvorsen, 2007)

At this point I began to realise how courageous all these people were - the ones who were researching vaccines and writing about their findings so that the public could make informed decisions. They spent years researching and documenting their findings, referencing all the facts that they wrote about. All the books that I read – and have refered to in this book - were, and are, fully referenced, so that the reader can go back to the original paper published. And yet these authors, many of them medical doctors, were and are, being attacked, either by their own governing bodies, often with the threat of losing their license to practise, or by the media purely for bringing the facts about diseases and vaccines to the public's attention so that we can make an informed decisions on our health. The other odd thing was that in all the attacks by the media, there were no references to back up their statements, no research that I could follow; just quotes from 'professionals'. Now that I was thinking for myself, it struck me as very odd that I had always just blindly believed these 'professionals'. I did not know them or what their qualifications were, other than the fact that most of them had MD after their name. I knew nothing about what qualified them to make the statements they did - that vaccines were necessary and safe. They had never proved to me that they had researched these topics independently and come to these conclusions themselves. In fact the more I looked into it, the more it appeared that they were actually just happy to reiterate information that had been given to them either directly or indirectly by the manufacturers of the vaccines. They quote things like "It has been scientifically proven" the same way one chants a mantra, but they never show this scientific proof, they never produce the data. We have all grown up knowing the following aphorism, "A lie told often enough becomes the truth".

Next I decided to look at polio. Truly a disease that I was terrified of; all I could see in my mind's eye when I thought of polio were the pictures that I had seen of children in leg braces and on crutches; worse still of the ones in iron lungs who could no longer breathe for themselves.

During my research into polio I found some interesting information, all of which can be found in the very informative book, *Dissolving Illusions* by Suzanne Humphries, MD and Roman Bystrianyk. Prior to the polio vaccine being introduced in 1955, there were many diseases and substances which produced the same paralytic symptoms as polio and that the doctors of the time had no means by which to differentiate between them: so all of them were lumped together under the diagnosis of polio. Among them were aseptic meningitis, enteroviruses such as Coxsackie and ECHO (enteric cytopathogenic human orphan virus), Guillain-Barre syndrome, transverse myelitis, arsenic and DDT toxicity, undiagnosed congenital syphilis, lead poisoning, limb paralysis caused by intramuscular injections, and hand, foot and mouth disease to name but a few. Prior to 1954 the World Health Organization's (WHO) criterion of diagnosis for paralytic poliomyelitis was, *"spinal paralytic poliomyelitis: signs and symptoms of non-paralytic poliomyelitis with the addition of partial or complete paralysis of one or more muscle groups, detected on two examinations at least 24 hours apart"* (Humphries, 2013) – no laboratory tests and no long term paralysis. Then after the introduction of the polio vaccination in 1955, the criteria changed in such a way that if there was no residual paralysis 60 days after the onset of the symptoms, it was not considered to be paralytic polio.

So, from this information, it would appear to me that before the vaccine a person only had to be paralysed for 24 hours to be diagnosed with polio, but after the vaccine they had to be paralysed for at least 60 days, big difference! What I had not realised before this, is that it would appear that the majority of cases of polio resolve by themselves, leaving no residual paralysis at all. I had always been led to believe that if someone got polio, that was it, they were paralysed and stayed like that for life. It turns out I was misinformed. Also, since 1955 it has become possible for doctors to tell the difference between many of these diseases, (such as Coxsackie virus and aseptic meningitis), so they no longer get diagnosed as paralytic poliomyelitis. In reality this means that, regardless of whether a vaccine was introduced for polio or not, the number of cases of polio was going to fall after 1955 anyway, purely because the criteria for diagnosing the disease had changed and differential diagnosis of different diseases became possible. (Humphries, 2013) So was this the only reason for the decline in polio or did the vaccine play a part?

First, I realised I needed to understand what polio was. Polio, or poliomyelitis, is a virus. In fact: *"To date there are at least 72 viruses of the same family of the original polio viruses that can also be found at the site of neurological damage in syndromes that are identical to paralytic poliomyelitis. We vaccniate against only three of these 72 viruses."* (Gunn, 2011)

These viruses are found in the stools and transferred by contact from person to person, but must enter the body through the mouth. It used to be called 'infantile paralysis' because young children and infants were more commonly the ones affected, as they are always using their hands and mouths to "taste" their surroundings.

*"Most people who get infected with poliovirus (72 out of 100) will not have any visible symptoms. About 1 out of 4 people with polio virus infection will have flu-like symptoms that may include – sore throat, fever, tiredness, nausea, headache, stomach pain. These symptoms usually last 2 – 5 days and then go away on their own."* (http://www.cdc.gov/polio/about/index.html)

According to the World Health Organization, *"one in 200 infections (0.5%) leads to irreversible paralysis. Among those paralysed, 5% to 10% (of the 0.5%) die."* (http://www.who.int/mediacentre/factsheets/fs114/en/)

In fact, it appears that polio only became an epidemic and started to cause paralysis in developing parts of the world in the 20th century. In underdeveloped communities it was seen that if the native population had been exposed to polio, none of them were paralysed. So why was it causing paralysis in developing countries? A question even Dr Albert Sabin, the inventor of the oral polio vaccine asked.

*"...the most important question: why did paralytic poliomyelitis become an epidemic disease only a little more than fifty years ago, and as such why does it seem to be affecting more and more the countries in which sanitation and hygiene, along with the general standard of living, are presumably making the greatest advances, while other large parts of the world, regardless, are still relatively unaffected?"* (Humphries, 2013)

It would appear that a conscious decision was made to ignore the above question; to not look for the cause of the increase in paralysis, just to try to develop a vaccine for the said paralysis.

*"The white man's diet of refined and processed foods with the resultant lack of vitamins, the environmental and agricultural poisons, and specific invasive medical procedures all contributed to the rise in susceptibility of people living in industrialized parts of the world. But*

*by the time those connections were made, disease-causing food was well ingrained in the modern palate. Medical advances were met with gratitude even though many of them were dangerous and overused. Refined sugar, white flour, alcohol, tobacco, tonsillectomies, vaccines, antibiotics, DDT, and arsenic had become financial golden calves that led humanity blindly down a spiral of disease and misery. Unfortunately, the paralysis was uniformly attributed to poliovirus infections which thus justified and prioritized vaccine research at all costs. Many thousands of people were needlessly paralyzed because the medical system refused to look at the consequences of these golden calves.....and concentrated solely on vaccine research."* (Humphries, 2013)

It is known that a person who contracts poliovirus infection is likely to be more severely affected if their diet is high in refined sugar and flour. Also, the symptoms caused from exposure to DDT are the same as those of polio and would have been impossible, in the 1940s and 50s when DDT was used (with gay abandon because it was incorrectly thought to be safe to use even around food), for doctors to distinguish between the symptoms of DDT poisoning and polio.

And today, we all know, or know of, people with ME or chronic fatigue syndrome, but what we do not know is that the viruses causing these are from the polio family. Or that indeed there are 72 of these viruses in the polio family and only three are vaccinated against. So we see symptoms of polio every day but do not realise it. (Gunn, 2011)

I could go on and on here about all the diseases that I looked up and for which I had given my children vaccines - pertussis (whooping cough), diphtheria and tetanus (given in the DPT or DTaP vaccine), tuberculosis (BCG vaccine), mumps, rubella (given with measles in the MMR vaccine), haemophilus influenzae type B (Hib vaccine). However, they have been written about by far more knowledgeable people than me, and in greater depth than I could ever hope to go into. Suffice to say that every disease I researched told a similar story: their morbidity (the incidence of the disease, or the amount of people catching that disease) and/or their mortality (the amount of people dying from the disease) were all falling before the introduction of the vaccines for those diseases. But do not just take my word for it, do your own research. I suggest the following as a good place to start: *Dissolving Illusions* by Suzanne Humphries, MD and Roman Bystrianyk; *The Truth About Vaccines* by Dr Richard Halvorsen; *Vaccines – This book could remove the fear of childhood illness,* by Trevor Gunn; and *Vaccination Voodoo – What YOU Don't Know About Vaccine* by Catherine J Frompovich.

So where was I now? Shell shocked and in limbo really. The childhood diseases that I had been terrified of letting my children catch appeared to be relatively harmless if my children were eating a nutritionally healthy diet and living a healthy lifestyle such as getting enough sleep, fresh air and having a reasonable standard of hygiene. The vaccines were at best questionable. They did not meet any safety protocols, were full of toxic materials, human and animal DNA, and all safety data available on them was produced by their manufacturers so totally biased!

Let me ask you a question. If I put the following into a glass - DNA and blood from an aborted human foetus, threw in a dash of formaldehyde, a drop of mercury, more DNA and blood, (this time from a monkey), a virus, a pinch of yeast, a drop of lactose, and peanut oil extract - gave it a stir with a spoon, thus inadvertently adding a few unrelated germs to the concoction, would you drink it? Of course not! You would think I was completely off my rocker to even suggest it; what poison! In fact, I might even be prosecuted for attempted murder if I did so. Yet these are only some of the ingredients contained in vaccines, which we never question injecting into our beautiful children or ourselves.

And now for the biggest deceit of all.

# Chapter 16

I started to tell people what I had learnt. The amazing thing was that most of them refused to hear what I was saying. In fact, they called me a "conspiracy theorist". They refused to believe me when I told them that I knew Ariana acted the way she did as a result of vaccine damage because I had seen her change completely in the week after her vaccine. According to them, I was apparently completely delusional when I told them that I strongly suspected that Cole's type 1 diabetes was also related to changes caused in him by vaccines. I tried to tell them a little of what our lives were like on a day to day basis but it was too painful to open up, to tell them of Ariana's struggle to continue living, without becoming emotional or angry if they dismissed me or, worse, the children. I wanted them to realise how incredible strong and brave the children were in dealing with all that was going on for them, to understand that I had put hundreds, if not thousands, of hours into researching and that we were entitled to live our lives in the way we wanted based on my research and not follow a doctrine that we felt was flawed.

Let us look at the definition of conspiracy theorist. It is a person who holds a conspiracy theory which is defined as, *"a belief that some covert but influential organization is responsible for an unexplained event."* (The New Oxford Dictionary of English, 1998)

So, was I just a theorist who believed that an influential organization (the pharmaceutical and healthcare industries) was responsible for an unexplained event (Ariana's complete change in personality from "normal" to "autistic spectrum")? No, because my "belief" is now a proven fact as of August 2014. That is the date that Dr Brian Hooker of the Focus Autism Foundation, published a study in the peer-reviewed scientific journal *Translational Neurodegeneration* (Hooker, 2014) showing that the U.S. Centers for Disease Control and Prevention (CDC) censored key data linking the MMR vaccine to autism. What made him look at the statistics was the following:

A whistleblower from the CDC, William Thompson, a Senior Scientist with the CDC (Centers for Disease Control and Prevention), told Dr Brian Hooker that the 2004 study, which has been quoted repeatedly by the CDC as proof that vaccines are safe and do not cause autism, was deliberately manipulated to hide the fact that vaccines can and do cause autism. The study was published under the title "Age at First Measles-Mumps-Rubella Vaccination in Children With Autism and School-Matched Control Subjects: A Population-Based Study in Metropolitan Atlanta", in the journal Pediatrics. Before the data was manipulated, it showed that African American boys who received the MMR vaccine at three years of age or younger were 340%, that's right, 340%, more likely to develop autism than other children. For some reason, the rate of autistic regression in black children is reported to be twice that in white children. (Hooker, 2014)

Learn more about this at the following website: *http:// www.naturalnews.com/046566_autism_MMR_vaccine_CDC_ whistleblower.html#ixzz3BFC7Low9.*

In a statement issued by William Thompson's lawyers, MorganVerkamp LLC, on their website *http://www.morganverkamp. com* he says: "*...I regret that my coauthors and I ommitted statistically significant information in our 2004 article published in the journal Pediatrics. The omitted data suggested that African American males who received the MMR vaccine before age 36 months were at increased risk for autism. Decisions were made regarding findings to report after the* *data were collected, and I believe that the final study protocol was not followed. ...There have always been recognized risks for vaccination and I believe it is the responsibility of the CDC to properly convey the risks associated with receipt of those vaccines."* (Thompson, 2014)

Interestingly, the researchers Drs Frank DeStefano, MD, Marshalyn Yeargin-Allsopp, MD, and Coleen Boyle, PhD, who hid this truth for the last 10 years, were all employees of the CDC whose trade mark, by the way, is "saving lives, protecting people." *(http://www.cdc.gov/)* Drs Frank DeStefano, MD, Marshalyn Yeargin-Allsopp, MD, and Coleen Boyle, PhD In fact, Dr Coleen Boyle testified before the Oversight Committee on Government Reform in recent years to the effect that "vaccines and their components did not increase the risk for autism." *(https://www.youtube.com/watch?v=uNWTOmEi_6A)* So, the study in which she participated, showed a link between the MMR and autism, and she and her co-authors on the study and high ranking officials within the CDC decided to manipulate the data and hide it from the public. Why? Presumably, because it did not tally with what they were telling the public. If I knew that something I was selling to the public could cause them harm and I covered that up and it was later found out, I would be brought to trial and I would probably go to prison. Interestingly after this manipulation of data, Coleen Boyle was given the job of CDC's Director of National Center on Birth Defects and Developmental Disabilities. *(http://www.cdc.gov/ncbddd/AboutUs/biographies/Boyle.html)* Frank DeStefano, until recently, held the job of Director of the CDC's Immunization Safety Office and Marshalyn Yeargin-Allsopp held the job of Medical Epidemiologist and Branch Chief, of the Developmental Disabilities Branch, Division of Birth Defects and Developmental Disabilities of the CDC. *(http://www.cdc.gov/employment/pdf/Job_Profile_Pediatricians.pdf)* These are all people who altered the data because it did not suit them, regardless of the fact that thousands, possibly millions, of children would be at risk and come to harm. And what of the former head of the CDC at the time, Dr Julie Gerberding? Well, she went on to be employed by Merck, one of the pharmaceutical manufacturers of the MMR vaccine, among others. *(http://www.mercknewsroom.com/news-release/ corporate-news/merck-announces-appointment-dr-julie-gerberding-executive-vice-president)*

In their press release, Focus Autism says:

> *"According to David Lewis, PhD, former senior-level microbiologist with the US Environmental Protection Agency's (EPA) Office of Research & Development, skewing scientific data to support government policies should be considered a major problem at federal agencies, including EPA, CDC, and USDA. Lewis, who was terminated by EPA after publishing papers in Nature that questioned the science the agency used to support certain regulations, believes top-down pressure on federal scientists and researchers working on government-funded projects in academia jeopardizes public health.*

> *"I've found working for the government is no different than working for corporations. You either toe the line or find yourself looking for another way to make a living," Lewis says. "No one would be surprised if Merck published unreliable data supporting the safety of its products. Why would anyone be surprised that the CDC or any agency would publish skewed data to conclude that the vaccines it recommends are safe? Scientists need a better system, where scientists are free to be honest." Accordingly, Focus Autism suggests that the CDC be held accountable to release all vaccine safety data in order to allow for independent, unbiased analysis." (http://www.thecoli.com/threads/parents-cdc-whistleblower-says-mmr-shot-raises-autism-risk-in-african-american-babies-3-n-under.243392/)*

Please note what Mr Lewis is saying. He is confirming what I have been trying to tell people - that if you work for a company, be it either a pharmaceutical company or a government agency, if you do not follow the official company/government policy you are out of a job. He also says, *No one would be surprised if Merck* (one of the major pharmaceutical companies and vaccine producers) *published unreliable data supporting the safety of its products.* Well, I think that some of you reading this book may be surprised. You may also be horrified when you remember that this is the safety data which your doctor and your government's health agency are basing their beliefs on when they tell you that all vaccines are safe for your child and you.

Actually, what is being covered up, glossed over and not told to you is that scientists within these companies are coming foward and blowing the whistle on the fraudulent and dangerous goings on within these companies. In 2010, two former Merck scientists filed a False Claims Act in the US stating that Merck had lied about the safety and efficacy of the MMR vaccine and had tampered with the results of its tests for several decades (Krahling and Wlochowski v. Merck, 2010). They then used these false results to claim that their vaccine was safe and effective. Did you hear about this from your government? Your doctor? The mainstream media? No, you did not. Why? Could it be that they are all biased towards the drug companies? Quite possibly. A lot of them have either direct ties to or are dependent on funding from drug companies. *(http://www. naturalnews.com/048402_measles_vaccine_scientific_fraud_court_ documents.html)*

Did you know that in the US you are not allowed to sue drug companies for vaccine damage? This is because of the National Childhood Vaccine Injury Act of 1986. Then again in 2011 the Supreme Court, in the Bruesewitz v. Wyeth LLC, decided that, while it recognised that vaccines were unavoidably unsafe, it chose to safeguard the multimillion drug companies over the public. *(http:// www.supremecourt.gov/opinions/10pdf/09-152.pdf)* Interesting, isn't it? They admit that vaccines are "unavoidably unsafe", and therefore can cause harm, yet governments and doctors continue to tell the public, you and me, that vaccines are completely safe, and we are bad parents if we do not get our children vaccinated. Yet there is a system in the US called The National Vaccine Injury Compensation Programme (NVICP) which was set up in the 1980s, and through which, by 2010 the US Court of Claims had awarded nearly $3 billion dollars to vaccine victims. *(http://www.nvic.org/injury-compensation.aspx)*

In fact, all of the following developed countries also have vaccine damages compensation schemes; since the 1960s France and Germany; since the 1970s Denmark, Switzerland, Japan, Sweden, New Zealand, England and Austria; since the 1980s Finland, Quebec and Taiwan; since the 1990s Italy, Republic of Korea and Norway; since the 2000s Hungary, Iceland and Slovenia. *(http://www.who.int/bulletin/volumes/89/5/10-081901/en/)* Of noticeable absence are Australia, Canada and Ireland.

The fact that all these countries have vaccine damages compensation schemes and pay out damages, in my humble opinion, makes a complete lie out of what the public is told - that "vaccines are completely safe."

There is no independent, free or honest research easily available to you, just what the pharmaceutical companies are paying for. There is independent research which has been carried out and questions vaccine safety, yet we the public are never told about it. In fact, I doubt very many GPs even know about it. In a paper published by researchers at the University of British Colombia titled "The vaccination policy and the Code of Practice of the Joint Committee on Vaccination and Immunisation (JCVI): are they at odds?", you can clearly see that there are independent studies, and that they have been submitted to the JCVI, who, instead of looking into them thoroughly (as they question vaccine safety), chose to ignore them totally. The researchers show that health authorities, pharmaceutical companies and vaccine manufacturers have known about the dangers of giving multiple vaccines at one time but have chosen not to tell the public in order to maintain "herd immunity." *(http://nsnbc.me/wp-content/uploads/2013/05/BSEM-2011.pdf)*

"Herd immunity" is thrown around with gay abandon; especially as an accusation to those of us who now choose not to vaccinate our children. We are blamed for not maintaining it; it is our fault if diseases do not disappear. Well, let's clear up something here. "Herd immunity" is a hypothesis, a theory, a belief that was put forward in 1933 by a chap called Dr A.W. Hedrich, before mass vaccination programmes for measles were available. He had observed measles outbreaks over the previous 30 years in his community and he noted that if 68% of the population caught measles by natural infection, the other 32% of the population appeared to be protected and did not catch it. A theory by one person is all "herd immunity" is. (Hedrich, 1933)

Not a fact. It has never been re-observed in a community who have not been vaccinated, and it has most certainly not ever been proven in a vaccinated community, because, as we all know, no matter how high the rate of uptake for the measles vaccine, measles is still very much around and can be caught by those who are vaccinated. What you may not be aware of is that China has an almost perfect uptake of the measles vaccine (99%), and yet measles still exists and occurs in China. *(Difficulties in Eliminating Measles and Controlling Rubella and Mumps: A Cross-Sectional Study of a First Measles and Rubella Vaccination and a Second Measles, Mumps, and Rubella Vaccination www.ncbi.nlm.nih.gov/pmc/articles/PMC3930734/)* So the vaccine has not stopped individuals catching measles. That would suggest it is not effective, would it not?

In its *Global Manual on Surveillance of Adverse Events Following Immunization* the WHO states, "Herd immunity <u>theory</u> **proposes** that, in diseases passed from individual to individual, it is difficult to maintain a chain of infection when large numbers of the population are immune." (WHO, 2014) The emphasis is mine but you can see that it is not known, it is not a fact; it is a theory and it is proposed. According to the Oxford English Dictionary, to propose something is to put forward something for discussion or consideration by others. Also, you will note that the WHO uses the word "immune" and not vaccinated. Again, this is important because it has not been proved to be the case for vaccinated populations.

Now, here's the kicker. This hypothesis of "herd immunity" is based on a population catching the wild form of measles naturally, breathing it in through their nose and mouth, with their body's immune system responding to it the way it was built to do so. Vaccines are not natural and they bypass about 80% of the body's primary immune response system.

When I understood how the body's immune system worked, I began to realise why it is never a good thing to bypass 80% of it. In very basic and simplistic terms, the description is this: most natural viruses or bacteria enter the body through the nose or mouth, which are attached respectively to the trachea and thereby the lungs, or the oesophagus which leads into the stomach, then the small intestine, the large intestine and then out through the anus. Only when something breaks your skin does it have access to your blood, organs, tissues and so on. The aforementioned pathways are effectively "outside" of your body and are the respiratory, digestive and urinary tracts. For things to get into your body from here, they must cross membranes. Your body works very hard to stop that happening if it views something as toxic. Once the body recognises a potential poison in its system, it causes us to vomit and have diarrhoea in order to try to eliminate the poison. If that does not work, it causes an inflammatory response by sending an army of white blood cells to the area of toxicity, where they digest the toxin, and again, your body vomits and has diarrhoea to get rid of the waste product. The whole point of this is to try to keep the toxins out of your bloodstream. Examples of this are gastritis, sinusitis, laryngitis and cystitis. If this primary defence fails and the toxin crosses into the bloodstream, it is then up to the rest of your immune system. A lot of the time when this happens, but not always, the body produces antibodies, which do not destroy or eliminate anything, but merely act as a flagging system to indicate potential problems and to attract other elements of the immune system to the area to deal with it. Normally these toxins are then eliminated from the body via the skin and/or mucous membranes, causing rashes, as in measles.

Vaccines are injected into the body usually via an arm, leg or buttock and so completely bypass the first 80% of the immune system. We are told by doctors that we rarely see any vomiting, diarrhoea or rash from vaccines. Well, it would probably be better if we did, as it would mean that the body was at least mounting some sort of defence against those awful extras that you would never drink from a glass if I gave it to you - the DNA from human foetuses and monkeys, aluminium, formaldehyde, mercury etc. If we drank them we would probably have a better chance of getting rid of them without damaging ourselves because we would vomit and excrete them out. Anyway, once injected some of these substances (called "adjuvants"), supposedly stimulate the last 20% of your immune system into responding to the toxin of the bacteria or virus. The current medical system is delighted if they see antibodies produced. However, there are slight flaws in this way of thinking. Remember the rash that the body has when it is eliminating a naturally caught virus from the blood? Turns out this is very important. A Danish study published in *The Lancet,* 5th January 1985, showed that the absence of a rash increased the incidence of skin diseases, degenerative diseases of bone and cartilage, and certain tumours in adulthood. (Gunn, 2006) Also, guess what? There are no tests showing what these adjuvants do to the body in the short term, long term, separately or combined. Do they stimulate the immune system to respond and then conveniently stop? Or do they continue to annoy and aggravate the immune system, over taxing it and wearing it out, maybe? Is it possible that over time the immune system gets so tired or confused that it starts to attack itself? Could this be related to the rise in autoimmune diseases? Anything is possible. We do not know, because no one has researched it. Then the second flaw is that it is possible to have antibodies to a disease and not be immune to it. Equally, it is possible to have no antibodies to a disease and be immune to it. Trevor Gunn asked Dr John Clements leader of the WHO EPI (World Health Organisation, Expanded

Program on Immunisation), to comment on this in a letter in 1995 and his answer was,

> *"You are right to say there is not a precise relationship between seroresponse (production of antibodies) and protection... immunity can be demonstrated in individuals with very low or no detectable levels of antibody."* (Gunn, 2011)

So while I and many other parents have been ridiculed, ignored and treated appallingly, with an immense disrespect for our opinions, we have been right: the MMR vaccine is linked to autism. This of course begs the following questions: if one vaccine has been shown to be linked to an increase in the likelihood of getting autism, what about all the other vaccines; are they too causing damage both neurologically and physically; could the many diseases that are steadily increasing in today's world somehow be linked to the ever increasing number of vaccinations that children are being given? The medical profession and the pharmaceutical companies would like us to take their word for it that vaccines are safe and cause no harm; they want us to take it on "faith". It is not being researched freely or openly, and as we are now seeing, any research that does not agree with "vaccine faith" is being manipulated, squashed, withheld or ignored.

Not so long ago, the world was being told to take everything that the Church told them was true, on "faith". If they did not, and questioned things, they were persecuted, tortured and ridiculed. Remember the inquisition? For instance, the Church did not like it when Galileo said that the Earth revolved around the Sun, so in 1633 he was placed under house arrest where he remained for the rest of his life; and they banned and burnt his books. The masses were told that the Church and its priests were only acting in their best interests and that everything they said was true. Well, we all know how well that worked out: massive abuse both physical and mental, and many deaths. Indeed, we are still dealing with the repercussions today. So why does another institution, the medical profession, and the industries behind it (pharmaceutical, health and government) think we, the masses, should take them on "faith"? If their vaccines and drugs are so wonderful they will stand up to being scrutinised, examined and questioned. We have a right to freedom of thought, speech and belief. We have a right to all information and to make our own informed decisions. We have a right as to what we eat or inject into our bodies.

In saying that the way in which the Church has behaved is bad, and that some of those within the spiritual organisations, who held positions of power and trust, abused their positions and caused harm to many people, it does not mean that I am anti-spirituality. I am not. In the same way, just because I am questioning the safety of vaccines and drugs it does not mean that I am either anti-science or anti-allopathic (conventional) medicine. I am not. However, I do believe that some people within these establishments, who are in positions of trust and power, have and are abusing these positions and have caused, and continue to cause, harm to many people.

The definition of *"science"* is, *"the intellectual and practical activity encompassing the systematic study of the structure and behaviour of the physical and natural world through observation and experiment"*. (The New Oxford Dictionary, 1998)

This definition is important, as it says that for people to be scientific they must systematically study things using observation (what they see) as well as experimentation. As you have seen in our story to date, I have yet to meet a doctor or skeptic, who when it comes to vaccines, has been willing to listen to my observations of my child's reactions. I (and this has been the experience of a lot of parents), have been ridiculed, ignored and threatened when I have given my observations of how my child changed dramatically in the week after receiving one of her vaccines. Not really very scientific behaviour on their part, is it?

I believe that everyone has the right of access to all information so that we can all make informed and safe choices. I am not a tree hugger or some ditsy, whacky, conspiracy theorist. I am a rational, thinking person, who chooses to inform myself about how I live and what I put into my, or my child's body. Yet there are several dichotomies in our lives. While we would rather use anything natural over synthetic medicines, if at all possible, Cole is now completely reliant on synthetic insulin. Without it he will die. If he had been born just over 80 years ago and come to have type 1 diabetes, he would have died, as there was no synthetic insulin available then. So I am incredibly grateful to science for that. However, I believe that we are doing something environmentally that increases the risk of children getting type 1 diabetes, and in Cole's case I believe that, by giving him vaccines, something altered in his body that caused his body to develop an autoimmune disease. I am not alone in this belief.

Could it be that the ever increasing number of vaccines given to our children is a contributing factor to developing type 1 diabetes? Of course it is possible; but we will not know until it is scientifically examined without prejudice, and as of yet no one is looking for the cause or causes, only for a cure. While I would personally love to take Cole's diabetes away from him (what mother would not?), how much greater would it be to stop children actually getting this awful health challenge, that threatens not only their lifespan but the quality of it, in the first place? Pretty damn amazing, I would say. I, as a parent of a child with type 1 diabetes, would not wish it on anyone else, ever. So you might be interested to know that currently listed as an "Adverse Reaction" under the Endocrine System of Merck's MMR 11 vaccine is "diabetes mellitus", better known as type 1 diabetes. (Merck, 2014) So give your child a vaccine to supposedly stop them getting childhood diseases, that most of my generation got and survived happily as children, and in a trade off run the risk of having type 1 diabetes, which I can assure you is hell, hmm?

# Chapter 17

So much information! Most of the time my brain felt as if I had stuck my finger into an electrical socket and that instead of electricity flowing through me, I was downloading a complete set of new data; stuff I had never heard of before, yet all of which had been around for many years. And all the time our everyday life continued.

Ariana was still having major challenges just trying to deal with the social aspect of life, let alone trying to cope with school work, and Cole wished to be let go to boarding school the following September. Yikes! Such a scary thought that I would not be on hand to keep him safe, but I had always aimed to bring our children up to be independent and loving individuals, so I knew that no matter how scared I was at this prospect, or what it cost me emotionally, I would let him go. So I was juggling trying to keep Ariana from deciding to quit this world while trying to master the insulin pump, (which was magic in what it could do, but was still only a machine, so could only work with the information I programmed into it; if I got it wrong I could still overdose or deprive him of insulin; still kill him) so Cole could leave me on his road to independence; while at the same time trying to find time for Théa so she did not feel abandoned and unloved.

And Nicky, you may ask? Well, by now I was spread so thin that I had nothing left to give to him. Relationships only work if you put effort into them, and I could not anymore. Nicky, for his part, had never known how to as far as emotional input went. I had always done all the emotional leg work in our relationship. We could have loads of fun doing things if I could leave any emotional pulls aside. In the beginning of our relationship, I could. I was happy with that, knowing that he loved me, enjoyed spending time with me and we did things together such as diving and building our house; physical things. He was just lousy when it came to complex emotional stuff. But now circumstances had changed me, I needed more. I needed emotional support from him and he was not in a position to give it. It was not his fault, though it took me a long time to understand this, so I was angry with him a lot of the time. We never yelled or ranted; it just was not how we were, or the atmosphere I wished our children to grow up in. And perhaps anger is the wrong word. It was more like a let-down feeling or an incredible irritation when yet again he disappeared to work and left me all alone to try and save our family with no emotional back-up.

Then his parents "retired" and became "consultants" to the business, and a whole new world of challenge opened up to us. Nicky now had three jobs to do. What little time he had been able to give us before was completely taken up, and now, along with going to work at 7a.m., he rarely came home before 11p.m. He worked and survived. I kept our family together and struggled with the loss of my friend, my lover and occasionally, I wondered about my sanity.

We have friends who when something breaks in their house, the wife says, "I bet Nicky could fix that" and the husband silently curses Nicky under his breath. When I first came to live here, I met an incredibly gifted person who referred to Nicky as "f***ing action man" every time we would meet. How he told the story was that he had spent hours helping his father to try and recover a lost mooring for a boat, sweating away and receiving little thanks for his efforts, when his father decided to call Nicky and ask him for help.

"Well, there I was taking a well-earned breather after hours of effort. Trying to recover my breath when up rolls 'f***ing action man' in his Land Rover. He opens the back, takes out all his diving gear, strolls down to the waters edge, dons the gear and hops in the water. I'm thinking, 'Off you go mate, we'll see you when your air runs out,' but no. Within minutes he's back on the surface with the bloody mooring. My father sang his praises for the rest of the day, with no thanks to me for my effort; bloody 'f***ing action man'."

Yet there is a common thread to these stories and the people who are part of them. They all like Nicky. Even when he is being "f***ing action man", there is no rancour or dislike of him, just his talents! It is not possible to dislike someone who is happy to help out anyone whenever they need it and who does so simply because it is the right thing to do so, to be a Good Samaritan; he gets enormous satisfaction out of being able to make a difference. So I found it incredibly hard to accept that he could not help me, that action man was not wading in to help. Nicky, who can do, fix and invent anything – Cole used to bring his friends' toys home from school for Nicky to fix – knows nothing about Cole's insulin pump. He does not know how to programme it, how to run tests on Cole's insulin usage so that he has the information with which to do the programming, how to work out ratios to tell you how many carbohydrates of food one unit of insulin covers, or by how much one unit of insulin will lower high blood sugar readings. In fact, he knows incredibly little about how to make a functional difference with either type 1 diabetes or Asperger's. It is only now, years down the line, that I think I understand why this is so. He is furious with himself, and feels that he has failed his children, whom he loves very much. He cannot believe that he never looked into vaccines before giving them to his children. He who, when he meets anything new, examines it thoroughly until he understands in minute detail how it works, just blindly believed the doctors who said that vaccines were safe and the way to go. And here is the crux of it - because he has not been able to forgive himself, he has not been able to face either condition, so has not been able to learn about them either, and so cannot help me.

Believe me, I know all about guilt and how to use it to beat oneself up with. I did it for a very long time, but then I came to realise that I had done, and always do, the best that I can at the time with the information and skills that I have at that time. I also realised that the only way forward was to apologise to my children, to forgive myself and move on. I could not help them if I stayed in that state, making myself ill. But it was, and is, easier said than done. I did apologise to the children, and when we are struggling with diabetes or Asperger's, I apologise again for any part I may have played in them acquiring these conditions. Most of the time I can forgive myself, but when they are or I am struggling because of these conditions, I cannot help but wish that I had known then what I know now. But then, as Cole said the last time I had this conversation with him, "But maybe we would not be the people we are now if we had not had to meet all these challenges, maybe we are better and stronger and can help others."

And I look at my Phoenix, the live one, and I know that we can make it; we can survive, choose the course of our lives and make a positive difference to this world.

I know this; however it is still hard on days like today for instance, when Ariana is sad and wondering how to deal with the world. Both she and I think, not again, please not again. We can both see how far she has come, how much better she is than before, but what everyone else on the outside does not realise is that when you have a challenge, or your child does, if you have a bad day, it is not just that one bad day you are having to deal with; every other bad moment that is related in any way comes gate-crashing in on top of you and you have to fight hard not to be overcome. I am much better now at remaining positive because my children are so much happier than before, but there have been times when my "glass" of positivity has fallen over and all my positivity has spilled out and I have watched it disappear rapidly between the cracks in my life. On those days I have found that sitting under the shower is a very good place to have a cry: the children are less likely to hear me over the running water, and when I do eventually pull myself back together, I can blame my red eyes on getting shampoo into them. In the meantime, the water cascading over me is very soothing and warm. All I have to hope for is that the hot water does not run out before my crying does!

By now Nicky's and my relationship was so very rocky. I still loved him. Well, if I concentrated hard and breathed for a moment, I could remember what loving him was like, way back when we had time to spend together. Now we seemed to just pass each other at odd moments in life. He spent most of his time at work, weekends included, and I spent my time mostly with the children or researching how to help them, and sporadically seeing clients for homeopathic consultations. Weekends were when we saw most of each other because the children were home and I would try to do family things, like having meals together so we could all just try to catch up and be a loving family. And we were at those times. We would, and still do to this day, sit around the dinner table and laugh about things and have a lovely time together.

This is when everyone gets to hear the funny things that happen to each of us. Such as the time that Cole's teacher in the Steiner school handed me a book of stories written by the children in the class, all roughly 10 years old, and explained that it was done for the parents and that I could take it home for the night but to please bring it back the next day so that it could continue the rounds. He then smiled at me and said that Cole's story was quite unique. Immediately he said this I felt the first tingling of apprehension begin in my body but I smiled, thanked him and took the book wondering just how "unique" Cole's story could be? He was into dragons and magic at that time, so it was probably along those lines and perhaps a little gory with people being eaten very descriptively, or maybe some overly imaginative magic spells.

I started to read the book and the stories were what I expected of that age group; magic, foreign lands, knights, princesses, wars and the like, so I was lulled into a sense of false security, totally unprepared for Cole's contribution. With a fascinated horror I read his story which was very short, graphical and to the point. It went something like this:

"The girl woke up to hear her boyfriend screaming. It chilled her blood. She could not see him but all around her there were hooks and knives and blood and a big cross.

"She got free and ran out of the shed and down the road. Soon a car came along the road and she stopped it but the man that got out of the car was the same one that had stopped the night before to help her and her boyfriend when their car had broken down. She knew she was going to die."

At first I just stared at the story, thinking that all the other parents were going to read it, or in some cases had already done so, and they were definitely going to wonder about what kind of upbringing Cole was having! Then I just started to laugh and laugh until tears streamed down my face. In fact, I probably snorted, and snot was undoubtedly present because when isn't it if your crying? But suddenly I just felt incredibly liberated. I became aware, that to be perfectly honest, I just couldn't give a toss what the other parents thought of me. It was the least of my worries when I thought about it. Who cared? Certainly not me, not anymore, never again. However I was curious. I always am and I knew that he had not watched anything inappropriate on television because I vetted all that, so I was extremely interested to know where he had got this from.

When I asked him he said, "It was one of Kimie's ghost stories, but I only wrote a little of it because we had to do it in our best writing and so I was bored because it was taking to long." Thank goodness for laziness! Heaven knows how the rest of the story went. Kimie is my youngest sister, and at 15 years younger than me she is closer in age to Théa than to me. She has always adored my children, and they her, and loved playing with them. When they were young, she too was still young enough to be oblivious to all but them, to the extent that on occasion I would turn around in a shop to find that while I had been shopping they had all just sat down on the floor and set up house while, customers and staff alike, were all having to pick their way around or over them. That night I asked Théa about the ghost stories.

"Théa, you know these ghost stories that Kimie tells you when she visits? I always thought they were along the lines of old fashioned folk tales; you know like, 'The lady in grey floated along the corridor and disappeared through the wall, etc.' "

"Well, they were in the beginning but then we had heard all of them, so she got more imaginative and I think that she uses the plots from horror movies she has seen as their base line."

Well, we certainly livened up the rest of the parents' days when they read Cole's story. They probably gave thanks that it was not their child and congratulated themselves that they, in fact, were actually doing far better at parenting than his parents!

I honestly believe that Nicky and I are still together because I eventually stopped trying to change him. What I grew to realise is that it is not Nicky's job to make me happy, that my happiness should not be reliant on how he or anyone else acts. I am the only one in life who can make me happy. When I realised this I stopped blaming him for things. Sure, he still did and does do things that bug me, as I know I do for him, but he is kind and loving and when he is in a good place, funny. He listens to everything that I propose to try to help our children and family have a happy life and, apart from the fact that every time without fail (he cannot help himself), he will point out our lack of finances, he never tries to stop me. He has always known that I have thoroughly researched ever option currently known to me, and is happy that if I feel our children may benefit from something then that is good enough for him. So he could not support me emotionally, and yes it was tough, extremely tough, but I survived, adapted and am happy. But do not doubt for a moment that there were several times over the last seventeen years when either one or both of us wondered whether it would not be better to call time on our marriage.

Turns out we are not alone in this. It is estimated that around 80% of marriages that involve a child with a challenge do not make it. What I can say now is that we are happy to be together at this moment, but I cannot promise that it will be forever; it is a work in progress. What I know for certain is that I do, and always will, love Nicky; but loving and liking, as I have always told our children, are two different things. Love is what I strive to act with and feel for all humanity; liking is a whole different ball game. There are many things that I do not like, namely lying, manipulation and the like.

# Chapter 18

So Ariana was now 14 years of age, had a diagnosis of Asperger's and so far nothing had been able to help her; not allopathic (conventional) medicine, homeopathy or any other discipline that I had tried. To be fair, every time I or another homeopath treated Ariana, the remedies would work for a very short time, such as a week at the most, and then stop. Each time, my hopes would start to rise, I could not help myself, (I am her mum!), only for them to plummet when yet again life became a constant battle of survival for her and us. But it did get me wondering if there was something blocking anything from working. For instance, homeopathy worked on the rest of the family, just not Ariana. So I again began trawling the internet for options, and I found something that would be life changing for Ariana and us. A Dutch, medically trained doctor, who was also trained as a homeopath and choosing to practise as the latter, had been having a lot of success helping children on the autistic spectrum. His name was Dr Tinus Smits. He had written a book called *Autism Beyond Despair,* and there was a documentary made about his work. After reading the book, I contacted Dr Smits and went to train with him in his methods of using homeopathy to help children on the autistic spectrum.

In Dr Smits' experience, he had found that autism was an accumulation of different causes with about 70% of cases due to vaccines, 25% due to toxic medication and other toxic substances and 5% to some diseases. Using isotherapy, where homeopathy uses the causative substances themselves in homeopathic preparation, he was finding that it was possible for the body to erase the toxic imprints. He called his method CEASE – Complete Elimination of Autistic Spectrum Expression. (Smits, 2010) Please note, he did not say elimination of autism, but elimination of the expressions of autism.

I went into my studies with an open mind. So far it had been my experience that nothing had been able to help Ariana, and I was well aware that what worked for one person did not always work for another due to the complex and individual nature of each human being. I was also aware that if there was any physical damage in a person's brain, such as that caused by epileptic fits, or any malformation during development, that these were not going to be reversible. However, I knew categorically that my child had developed as expected until two years of age and had then changed, and changed again before my eyes at four years of age after her vaccination, so I knew in her case that she had been damaged by vaccinations.

I came home from the course with new hope and immediately started implementing my learning with Ariana. For us the results were startling and dramatic. Within three months Ariana no longer called me 20 times a day; just twice, in the morning and evening. While she still struggled to interpret her peers and teachers, she could comprehend my explanations of their behaviour. While she still saw the world in black and white, right or wrong, she could allow that others had grey shades, a lot of them, and that they did not always see misrepresenting the truth as "lying". Such as when a teacher says that the class is going to do one thing but then does something completely different with them. Or that they expect their pupils to behave in a certain way and punish some students if they do not while letting others away with it. Such lack of continuity and fairness is incredibly frustrating, even to me! Now, instead of just writing these people out of existence as she would previously have done, she allowed them to remain in her world. She did not trust them one bit, but could tolerate them in order to survive in the school and still attend their classes. It did not matter to me that it was highly unlikely that she would ever be able to learn anything with that particular teacher ever again because she no longer had any respect for them. What mattered to me was that she could now function within society without me being omnipresent. She could get up in the morning, follow a timetable, interact with her peers, last five days at school, and laugh occasionally. She became reasonably happy. Well, using the word "happy" is a bit of a stretch, but she was not crying all the time. It was amazing. I began to glimpse the child that had begun to slip away from me at two years of age. We all began to breathe more easily and dared to hope that life would get easier.

In the beginning, I still sat around all day like a cat on hot coals waiting for Ariana's phone calls. When she did call in the evening, the first thing I would ask was, "Are you happy? How did your day go?"

She would think for a minute and then say, "Well, I am better than before but I would not say happy. Happy would mean that I enjoyed being here, was having fun, which I am not." Then she would go through her day with me. There were still things that had happened in the day that had annoyed her, and she still had to talk them through with me in the evening, but she could wait to do so! You have no idea how huge this was. While she was not happy, she was able to cope and no longer wished to die. I no longer lived on tenterhooks all day, every day, wondering if today would be just too much for her to bear; if today was going to be the day that I truly lost my daughter; the day when she would decide that life was just too painful and not worth it.

Things continued to improve the more we used the CEASE method. It was not always easy, though. For instance, when we started to detox the Hib vaccine (this is the Haemophilus Influenzae vaccine and actually the name is a misnomer, H. Influenzae is not related in any way to influenza; first isolated by Pfeiffer during the influenza pandemic of 1890, it was mistakenly thought to be the cause of influenza). (Vermeulen, 2005) As the Hib vaccine began its detoxification from her system, she immediately produced the following symptoms: severe headache; her eyes felt as if they were being pulled out of her head; to move her head she had to close her eyes; sore neck; high temperature; her right ear felt as if it would burst; she felt very hot, then very cold; her skin was boiling to touch; her hands would feel hot and her feet cold or vice versa; she felt as if she was constantly on the verge of vomiting; lethargic; and bright lights hurt her eyes. It was absolutely terrifying as they were all the symptoms of meningitis, bar the rash. I sat with her all the while, treating her homoeopathically and feeding her high doses of both vitamin C (highly disliked by both viruses and bacteria alike, and if you take too much, you know because you get a dose of the trots, so you reduce it - very user friendly!) and vitamin D (activates the anti-viral potential of your immune system), and lots of water, and after 24 hours she was over the worst of it, just worn out. And yet part of me could not help but be amazed at the same time. Ariana had received her last dose of the Hib vaccine at 6 months old. She was 18 years old when we began this detox, and the minute we did, she produced known symptoms associated with the Hib bacterium, which can infect the outer lining of the brain causing meningitis. Was it possible that the bacteria from the Hib vaccine had lived in her system for the last 16 years? Back to researching for me!

Interestingly, I found several studies that showed that the measles virus was found to be living in the tissues of people with Crohn's disease many years after they had either caught the wild virus or been given the vaccination. (Meulen,1998) This article lists 26 papers on the subject. So it would appear that, yes, it was very possible that the bacteria from the vaccine could have lived in her body for that long.

Those with keen observational skills will have noticed here that I started the CEASE protocol with Ariana when she was 14 years of age and that the above episode happened when she was 18. Well, she is 19 now and we are only now almost finished with the detox. It has been a long haul. Mainly because it brought so much stuff up and out for her that we needed to take breaks in between so that both she and I could retain our sanity. But without question it has been worth it; incredibly hard but definitely worth it. Over all she is a different child/adolescent to the one we started with. She rarely has hissy fits, or spirals out of control, and no longer wishes to die because life is too hard to deal with. She now has periods of time where she is extremely happy. She knows what she wants to do with her life, and she can deal with all sorts of people and tolerate "idiots" or "unfair" people if the situation requires it. If things are starting to get to her she can take time out by taking herself off and doing something on her own. However, we know when we need to move on to the next detox because her body will throw wild symptoms at us, like the cough she got recently which she described as "if there was a coating all over the inside of my throat, stuck to it, like someone painted it on; it should not be there, it is not real and I want to scrape it off" – like a false membrane perhaps? Well, that is what diphtheria is, and seeing as how the cough was not responding to anything else and the DPT was the next vaccine in the detox schedule, I gave it. Within 12 hours the cough had gone, as had the "coating" feeling on the inside of her throat. Interesting, huh? However, as has happened to her often while following the CEASE protocol, she became very melancholy and depressed, eczema flared up, and she became extremely anxious, playing a less intense version of the "what if" game. She is extremely brave when this happens and will soldier on, but it is hard for her and she often wishes that this had never happened to her, that she had never got Asperger's. This is when I again offer my apologies for ever having vaccinated her, and point out how much better she is than previously in that she can now cope on her own in the world without me, and even function, most of the time, with the anxiety, and in general support her through it. Invariably she comes out the other side of it in a week or so, but it is extremely wearing for both of us, and we are a little bit ragged to say the least, on reaching the other side. Once she regains her strength, we all notice how much better Ariana is. She will have matured, grown stronger both physically and emotionally, will be more positive and happier than before, and much more able to cope with social situations; in fact looking forward to new situations, which was completely unheard of before!

At the same time as using the CEASE protocol with Ariana, I also tried it with Cole. I know, I know, he is not on the autistic spectrum, but I believe that he has been damaged by vaccines. I believe that there are enough doctors, scientists, parents and others raising the question that vaccines could be linked to the rise in type 1 diabetes (and as we have seen it is listed as an "adverse effect" for some vaccinations), for it to be ignored anymore. There are numerous studies on the link between specific vaccines, and vaccines in general, and their connection with type 1 diabetes. (Gunn, 2011) *www.thinktwice.com*

So I started to detox Cole, mainly because after he was diagnosed with type 1 diabetes, his immune system had been shot to hell. He would catch every single bug going and it would take weeks to get him over them. He would have just recovered completely from one to be taken out by another! But what those of you lucky enough not to be initiated into the club of "life with type 1 diabetes" do not get, is that a bug, any bug, be it vomiting or just one that causes sniffles, is a complete pain in the butt to someone with T1 (I'll call it that, if I can, from now on, because writing "type 1 diabetes" every time is beginning to irritate the life out of me). The "bug" messes up everything spectacularly and with ease; it is a royal spanner in the works. Blood glucose levels usually shoot up through the roof, usually before any outward sign of the bug manifests itself. So you constantly have to give more insulin to try to lower the glucose levels, but the kicker is that you never can be sure how much to give or for how long you will need to give it.

Think of a tyre with a slit in it, with the inner tube bulging out of it. You have no puncture repair kit, but you do have a wonderful new glue you can glue up the slit with, if you can get the inner tube back into the tyre. It is imperative that you do this because if you do not, the inner tube will burst and you will have a flat tyre. Now try to push that inner tube back in without letting out any of the air; even if you could, it would be impossible to keep it there and pull the slit together to glue it. So you let out a little bit of the air so you can push it back in and try to glue the slit, but if you let out too much air the whole tyre will collapse and you will still end up with a flat tyre. Well, it's a bit like that. You have to lower the high glucose readings or the person with T1 could end up in a coma, feeling very ill or do permanent damage to their blood vessels; but if you lower them too much they could also end up in a coma! The thing is, even if we do not eat anything at all, our body releases glucose from our stores of fat because it is imperative for our survival that the body has some glucose constantly swishing around in its system to function. So even if Cole felt ill and was eating nothing, he actually had to check his bloods more often than normal! How fair is that? Feeling yuck and having T1? Well, gee, you get the added bonus of sticking more needles into you than normal, trying to engage your brain in mathematical equations to work out your insulin needs, and the biggest bonus? You cannot just go to bed and sleep it off. Nope, it would be way too dangerous to ignore what your glucose levels are doing, remember the coma bit? So you get to either set alarms or wake yourself up if you are an adult, or if you are a child, you get your Mum sticking needles into you while you are asleep!

I cannot actually believe that I am going to say this, but I have actually got quite good at sticking needles into Cole while he is sleeping. It is not really an accolade that I want or am overly proud of, though. There is a trick to it; I want the needle to go deep enough into his finger to draw blood, but only just deep enough, as the deeper the more pain; and I want to do it fast, the faster the better, as it disturbs him less. I hold his finger gently but firmly, so that there is a pressure, as this seems to distract a little from the pain of the needle breaking the skin. Then, once the blood is flowing, I move like lightening to transfer it to the meter, as once disturbed, Cole of course has a tendency to turn over and pull his hand away from me. Now, with the pump, I just programme the correction into it and it delivers the insulin to him; but when he was on MDI (multiple daily injections) I would then have to work out the amount of insulin needed for the correction and inject it into him while he slept. Remember the 10 second hold at the end of the injection? Well, this lead to some fun antics: me pinning him down so that he would not turn over with the injection in him; his personal favourite - him farting in my face and me dying of asphyxiation and not being able to move because I had to wait for those 10 seconds; and my personal favourite - him opening his eyes, glaring at me and saying, "a horse could do it better than you", and promptly closing his eyes and going back to sleep! Oh yes, and remember all of this is usually done in the dark, or with the least amount of light possible, so as not to wake everyone up for the rest of the night.

Back to the detox. As far as I was concerned, the last vaccine Cole had been given was the MMR at two years of age so I started to detox that. Immediately, his eczema flared up to the worst it had ever been and appeared in places that it had not been before. Since he had got T1 he had had eczema around the backs of his knees and in the bends of his elbows. While it was always visible and a slight irritant to him, if his glucose levels were high it would flare, and at night while he was asleep he would scratch it raw and make it bleed. At times it would look as if someone had taken a knife to him and removed the top layer of skin. Now however, it reached new heights of horror. It appeared all over the front of his neck and looked as if someone had poured boiling water over him. I was both fascinated and appalled; fascinated that his body was responding to the detox and therefore, I believed, had been affected by the original vaccine in the first place, and appalled that he was going through such a reaction. I did all I had been taught on the CEASE course. When I was getting nowhere with that I used constitutional homeopathy but the best I could do was to calm it enough so it no longer drew attention like a beacon!

Then I had an "aha" moment. I remembered that when he had come out of hospital after being diagnosed with T1 he had been bitten in the face by the Rottweiler. Oh yes, I forgot to mention that to you too, didn't I? Well, that is because I tried very hard to forget it. Within the first week, yes the first seven days after our world had been turned upside down, Cole was bitten by a dog that he knew, in the face. To be fair to the dog, Cole climbed into its owner's van (thankfully into the front), and lent over the seats into the back to talk to the dog. The dog took exception to Cole coming anywhere near his master's tools, which lived in the back, and without warning – I know this because I, Nicky, the owner and several others were there watching, just outside the van – lunged forward and bit Cole full in the face. "Luckily" for us, the Rottweiler had previously been run over by a truck and lost half of his teeth so, whether it was that fact or, more likely, that the seats had been between Cole and the dog, he let go after biting Cole. Cole fell out of the front of the van screaming with Nicky and me already running towards him.

My belief in the core goodness of humanity is fuelled by the unsolicited actions of people. One of them happened here. A young guy on holidays, who just happened to be watching too, ran forward and offered his assistance as he was a nurse, (I think from Germany, not that it matters except that I never got to thank him properly for his kindness, so on the off chance that he reads this book, thank you). Anyway between Nicky and I, who are both trained in first aid, and the Good Samaritan, we treated Cole, calmed him down and Nicky rang our friend the doctor. Of course, this all happened on his half day, did you expect anything else? I bundled Cole into the car and met both doctors at the surgery, where they very kindly sewed Cole's face up. This they did at my behest, because I just could not face going back into hospital, the thought of it was akin to being sent back to a house of torture or jail; and because the dog was missing half his teeth, Cole had been "lucky", and there were only two deep cuts needing stitches, one from the outside edge of his right eyebrow extending down and out to the hair line in a perfect continuation of the curve of the eyebrow itself, and the other just under his right eye, and I mean just under it, beside his nose over the sinus cavity. In this day and age of suing, I know that we were fortunate indeed that our friend knew us and was happy that they could sew up Cole without risk of litigation.

But now comes the reason that I have buried this incident. Not because Cole could have been ravaged, killed or nearly lost his eye, no. Not because I had to pin my child to the bed, physically lie on him and clamp his face between my hands to hold him still so that he could be sewn up while he begged me to stop, no. It was because I was so traumatised by the diagnosis of T1 and Cole being bitten in the face by the Rottweiler that, when the doctor insisted that, in his opinion, it was necessary to give a tetanus injection due to the fact that the dog's teeth had probably penetrated Cole's sinus cavity, that I eventually caved and allowed him too. I, who at that time knew categorically that Ariana had been damaged by a vaccine; I, who knew that all research into vaccines was biased as it was carried out by their manufacturers; I, who knew that all the information the doctor had was from the manufacturer too and so biased, bowed to their belief and not mine, and allowed them to inject a toxin into Cole's body and his already struggling immune system. That is why I buried the incident and tried to forget it, because I could not believe I had done such a thing, and I had not forgiven myself.

When I had this realisation and faced my "bad moment" instead of trying to lock it away, I realised that the last vaccine Cole had been given was the DPT (diphtheria/pertussis/tetanus) or the DT (diphtheria/tetanus). Because tetanus vaccine on its own does not have a very long shelf life, the manufacturers always put it with diphtheria vaccine or pertussis and diphtheria vaccine. So I started to run a detox with him for the last vaccine received, and like magic his eczema started to disappear within days of starting the detox and was gone a couple of weeks later and it has never returned. Not only that, but I noticed over the next few months that he was much healthier; he stopped catching every bug going, and if he did get a bug, he was able to recover as fast as the rest of us, which is still true today. Cole still has T1 but he is the healthiest T1 I know and that, I believe, is due to CEASE and regular homeopathy. Also, if his spirits get low (which would be termed depressed if we went to the doctor for it), and why would they not with all he is constantly having to face and remember to do just to live, homeopathy always helps him to come back to his normal optimistic, cheerful self.

I was, and still am, amazed by what Dr Tinus Smits' CEASE protocol has done for my children and others. I will be eternally grateful to this kind and generous man who gave so much to help others, who gave me the tools with which to rescue the daughter I had damaged. Is CEASE "the answer" for autism or the only way to detox? No, of course not; what works for one is not always "the one" that will work for everyone, but it has helped us and many others. Is "homeopathy" the only answer for illness? Again no, of course not. For instance allopathic medicine is exceptional for emergency/acute care. However, there are many other medicines such as traditional Chinese medicine, naturopathy, nutrition, and of course, homeopathy and others, which allow one to manage one's long term health in a much less toxic way. Of course, it is always down to personal choice and the right to make that choice. I personally would like to manage my health, and that of my children, where at all possible, with natural medicines that do not cause deadly side effects. I am happy to do the research and ask questions to find answers. However, if someone else would rather give away their choice, is happy to allow someone else to choose what is best for them and take synthetic drugs - often multiple drugs, because as one drug causes a side effect they are then given another to "deal" with that side effect and so on - that is their choice. Freedom of choice; no one person or body has the right to dictate how another should live. My choices are right for me; your choices are right for you.

# Chapter 19

I debated about whether or not I would tell you any more about me. I mean really tell you about me and how I feel and have been affected - the good, the bad and the ugly, as the saying goes. I balked at bearing my soul that much, but having talked already about our marriage and told you how it has barely hung on by the skin of its teeth, what the heck, I may as well tell it all. I also think that it is important. One of the reasons I am writing this book at all is because I want people to get a glimpse into our lives. What it is like to live with children with health challenges, and what it is like for those children. Because I have met so many people along the way that are so very lucky to have "healthy" children and who just do not "get" me or my children, or us as a family, and therefore, by default, any parent of a child with a challenge or indeed a person living with a challenge. I am either viewed as a complete hippy that lets her children do anything that they wish, or a complete control freak who wishes to know how her children are all the time. Well, I am neither; I am just a mother, who is doing her level best, in a situation for which the only script that society has written is to submit, accept and go under; a script that I refuse to use. I am not looking for your sympathy, but I thank you if you have felt any compassion during our story so far. I am looking for you to understand that we, and many others, cannot live within what you consider "normal" society parameters, and I am saying that I have the right to my beliefs about and choices about, what is "healthy" for our family. If my child's health is at risk, be it that Cole's blood glucose/sugar levels are low or high, that Ariana is having a meltdown, or that one of us is feeling like life is such rubbish that it just is not worth living, then I am going to stop and address that straight away. No matter what. And if that makes us late for school, miss school altogether, take time out or do whatever it takes to sort the situation or distract us and bring some fun back into our lives, then that is what I will do.

My nephew had some English homework to do; it was to put words in context by making a sentence out of them. One of the words was "punctual" and his sentence read, "My auntie Kelly is never punctual". This made me laugh so much because it is true and I make no excuses for it. I can be on time if I have to be, but it would want to be extremely important for me to put myself under such pressure. I am on time when life is good and everything is swimming along beautifully, but if life is throwing several curve balls to me at the time, then my eye is on the balls and not the time.

I am not alone with this and before I go on here, please remember that we are the lucky ones; you are getting a glimpse into the lives of a family with challenges but one who is lucky. Want to know why? Because my child, who is on the autistic spectrum, is on the end where she can speak to us, knows how to dress herself, and can attend to her own bodily needs, such as going to the bathroom and feeding herself, on her own. Now, because of all we have done through detoxing, getting the equipment that Cole needed and so much more, my children are capable of being independent. There are many families for whom this would be the dream. Their child is not toilet trained even as an adult, cannot feed themselves and can never be left alone because they do not understand danger – to the extent that all windows and doors are locked in the house so that they do not leave without anyone knowing. They are completely dependent on their parent/s.

So now imagine that you have a child like this and you need to go to a doctor's appointment. The appointment is scheduled for 4p.m., but every time you have been to the doctor's surgery before, you have had to wait for maybe half an hour or more. So this time you aim to arrive half an hour late because your child will never sit in a seat, always paces up and down in an agitated state, waving their arms about, and screeching or moaning, and you can see that the other patients are uneasy and afraid, or looking at you as if you are a bad mother and should be able to "make" your child behave in an acceptable fashion. However, this time when you arrive, the doctor is waiting on you for whatever reason (maybe someone else cancelled), and complaining because you are wasting his valuable time. He says things like, "I know things are hard for you but this is not acceptable". Well he knows nothing, unless he too has a child with a challenge.

No one knows how it is for us; only those who live similar lives to us. Not even our extended families "know" what our lives are like. And in the above scenario, the mother or father is usually afraid to answer the doctor. Afraid that if they start to try to tell them what their lives are really like, and how they really feel about it, that they will come away with antidepressants which they are afraid to take lest they cannot function 100% to mind their child; or that they will completely loose the plot and start to yell at the doctor and be accused of being abusive. If they started to tell what it was really like, they would probably not be able to stop for a very long time. And just maybe they are also afraid of being turned away from that doctor's surgery, or having social services directed to their door and having their already difficult life become 100 times worse, because then they would have to do as they were dictated to, while these children can never conform to a "one size fits all solution". So, you see, I am just offering you a glimpse of our lives here, not all of it, because I would have to right a trilogy or more to cover it. And maybe too much might frighten you or make you feel uncomfortable, so you would not finish reading this book; and the whole point would be defeated.

It is an odd thing, but some people are afraid of being too near children with challenges. It is as if they are afraid they may "catch" the challenge, or maybe the "luck" that that family is having. And it certainly makes a lot of people highly uncomfortable because they do not know what is expected of them. Well, I want to tell you that nothing is expected of you at all. All I, or any other parent wants, is for people to accept that we are different; to allow us our God (Universe) given right to lead our own lives, to decide what is right and safe for us and our families with regards to vaccinations, food, health, education; and not to be judged, scorned, ridiculed or worse, have our children taken from us. You think this is far-fetched? An exaggeration? Well go to *www.medicalkidnap.com* and see how many families lives have been ruined, children taken away from their parents because those parents wished to utilize less toxic healthcare choices; and remember, this is also happening outside of the US as well.

For the last seventeen years I have not had a full night's sleep. In the beginning, it was because Ariana was so upset that she could not sleep all night. Then it was because I was checking Cole's blood glucose/sugar levels during the night. Then, because Cole was at boarding school and trying to manage his bloods on his own, so many nights we would still be sorting out "highs" or "lows" till around midnight over the phone, or he would call during the night because he had become "high" or "low" and we would have to spend an hour or more sorting it out. Now, when Cole is really quite proficient at working things out for himself and wants to be more independent, it is because my body's sleep pattern has been so shot to hell that it cannot seem to recover. And of course, because I know that Cole is still going "low" or "high" some nights, just not calling me because he wants to do it on his own, rightly feeling that at 17 he is entitled to make his own decisions on how to manage his health, but I still wonder how he is - it is not possible for me to switch off that "Mum switch".

For several years now, Nicky and I have slept in separate beds because he snores and I sleep so lightly that I cannot deal with even the smallest amount of snoring. Actually not only separate beds, but separate rooms. Before I got married, I laughed at movies depicting the Victorian era where the men and women had their own rooms, or felt that, in the present day, there must be something highly wrong with a marriage/partnership if the couple did not share a bed every night. Not anymore. Now I know that it is the only way that we can survive, get some sleep and stay sane, because Nicky's snoring keeps me awake, then I wake him by making him turn over constantly! How I miss the closeness of always knowing that he is there with me at night: that if I wake upset or scared I can snuggle up to him and be reassured by his presence, that I am not alone. It amazes me how much I took it for granted in the early years of our marriage. When I now hear someone complaining that they have not gotten any sleep for a few nights because their child has been sick or they were upset over something, depending on how life is going for me, I either laugh to myself (on my good days), or restrain myself masterfully from telling them what sleep deprivation is really like (on my not-so-good days). It would be impossible for them to understand, because in order for them to do so I would have to tell them the whole story and that would take too long, and I would have to once again bare my soul to someone new.

Then there is the underlying fear, which is like a separate living, breathing entity inside me, always looking for an opportunity to break free of its bonds and take control of my life. In the beginning, the fear and I were in control in equal measure; it rained for half the time and I for the other half. But even when I reigned it was not a supreme reign: a lot of my energy was directed at keeping the fear under control. The fear was that Ariana would choose to kill herself rather than stay in a world that was so, well what? So intolerant of her? So alien to her? So unkind to her? So incomprehensible and demanding of her? All of these and more. Then the fear broadened, grew and became frantic to take over and rule my life all the time, as it now included Cole; that he too would stop trying to live after two years of being ill every day or that I would kill him by not getting his insulin right.

Now that Ariana and Cole are able to enjoy life, I reign, and the fear has gone to ground, only rumbling on occasions. But it is always there, running like an underground river deep in the background. It threatens to burst forth now most often in relation to diabetes. If Cole wishes to do new things, go new places by himself, be in situations that he has never experienced before and so has no idea how his body will respond and what he will have to do in turn to balance its demands for food and insulin, the fear whispers inside of me, "You cannot be there with him all the time; who will make sure that he is alright if you are not there? No one, he is on his own, and no one else knows what to do". He wants his independence, and that is what I want for him too, it is what is right, he is 17, but it is hard to let go. The following is from a diary that I wrote when he was 15:

*So now we are on holidays in the wilds of Connemara. It is beautiful, basic, rural and back to nature. The cottage has no electricity, just gas; no phones; no wifi; hot water is courtesy of a back boiler behind the fire which is constantly on during the day, burning turf with its own unique, earthy smell. We love it, right by the sea; at high tide the children – and I, because I cannot bare to miss out on any of the fun – go swimming, and as there are always loads of friends there is always loads of high jinks. There is a water trampoline which acts as a base onto which everyone tries to get, then push each other off. Masses of screaming, laughing teenagers and younger cousins, and of course a couple of adults who have never grown up! The children spend hours in the water, some in wet suits and some just in togs. It is freezing.*

*(If you have ever read Enid Blyton's Famous Five or Secret Seven you will have the picture - the children gone all day exploring, only returning when they run out of food!)*

*And so the other fun starts. The minute we arrive, Cole is far more active than he has been all year. If he is not messing about in the water with friends, he is on top of it in boats and canoes, or cycling or walking over miles of dunes and beaches. It is wonderful, he is so independent, exactly what I wish for and yet, nagging in some deep buried corner of my consciousness, a voice is screaming at me, "Are you out of your tiny cotton picking mind, woman?" Funny, it is always a masculine voice, this voice of fear – I, being female, am strong, like a woman from the fabled Amazon tribe (though I have no wish to cut off one of my breasts, as they did, to enable them to draw there bowstrings unencumbered!) Anyway, the fear comes, for instance, when Cole says that he and his friend are off over to the dunes to explore and play; an hour's medium-paced walk following the coast and visiting the four beaches on the way - exploring, seeing what treasures have washed up, long bits of ships ropes, buoys and so on, all things that have infinite possibilities when you are a teenage boy. They can be used to build bases, to tie your friend's and your legs together causing you to laugh hysterically when you try to walk and fall over flat on your face; to test each other's manhood, as only the strongest and most determined can haul and lug the thickest mooring ropes home over the miles of dunes because it is just right for mooring the raft that you made earlier. Such fun!*

*And yet a different scenario plays through my mind, alongside the one that Cole sees, the one I want him to see and do. I see hours of exertion, so I know that his metabolism will speed up and any insulin within his body will work much more efficiently. I see a teenage boy so caught up in the fun that he is having, that he does not want to stop to check his bloods to see what his body is doing, and does not want to have to think of and self regulate his bloods to stay safe and alive. I know that he will probably only check his bloods when he reaches the final destination on this walk, before they turn around to come home, or if his body is screaming out to him that it is "low" and causing his muscles to shake and making him feel nauseous.*

*So I smile at him and say that it sounds like a fun thing to do, and gently prompt him to bring his meter with him to check his bloods, and something to treat a low. He says that he already has them, and again, ever so nicely, because I am so aware that he is 15 and in his eyes I am nagging him and butting into his life, I ask what he has to treat a low. He says two cans of coke. So I praise him for having the foresight to put two cans in and not just one, and then I suggest that he might put in a third, and four mars bars as well! He rolls his eyes and I point out that he and his friend are always hungry – a by-product of being teenage boys and having stomachs like bottomless pits – and that I do not want them to reach their destination and only have the cokes for "lows" as snack food. This makes sense to him so he puts in the extra food. Then I gently remind him only to give himself half the insulin that he would normally if he is eating, because he is being so active, and he drawls, in a bored tone, "Yessss, Mum", impatient to be on his way.*

*These conversations are like complicated dance routines. We have them every time he wishes to do something on his own. My part of the dance is to try and state everything I want him to do and remember in order to stay safe, in the best way that I can so that he will hear me and not switch off, as teenagers have a tendency to do. His part is to try to pay attention and switch back on while I am talking so that he can leave quicker!*

*Then he's away, and I try hard not to know that part of his brain has already switched back off. I try not to see the worst case scenario. That he reaches the far off destination, suddenly hears his body screaming at him, "give me some sugar you prat! I am on the point of collapse here!" That he does indeed collapse before he can eat anything. That his friend, who in this case, thank you Universe/God, is a sprinter, sprints all the way home to me – half an hour. I then leap into the car and drive like a rally driver/maniac (think Cruella DeVil's driving in the animated version of 101 Dalmatians when she is looking for the escaped puppies) over the dunes, taking years off the life of the car, to reach where Cole has collapsed - another 15 minutes, therefore 45 minutes since his friend had to leave him all alone - only to find that he is not there. I would then feel the blood draining from my body and everything would feel like it was happening in slow motion. I would scout the area with the same friend, and anyone else who had come with me, in vain. Then I would have to assume that some Good Samaritan had come along and loaded him into their car and taken him to the nearest doctor. So I would start to call the police, the local hospital, the doctors. And here I have to stop the scenario, because if I go any further in my imagination, I will burst into heart-broken sobs because my body is already responding in terror like a mother who loses her child. I feel ill and tense and have a physical pain in my chest, as if someone has reached in and tried to rip my heart out.*

*So now I make myself see Cole's smiling face as he set off, laughing with his friend. I focus really hard on that laugh and then I busy myself, though I get nothing done because I cannot concentrate too well, for the next FOUR hours. I resist the urge just to "drive by" and check on him, only because I would not ever be driving by where he has gone; it is a destination, not a drive-by and so it would be oh so obvious to him. Then he arrives back at the agreed time, a minor miracle in itself, as he sometimes "forgets" the time too, and I smile and ask how his adventure was. I do not, as I wish to, fling myself onto him and hug him tight and kiss him and make him come sit with me, oh no, I am the epitome of calm and collected, and act as if life is just one big easy-going party at which I am constantly having a ball!*

I have come to love the following saying, "Fear is only the boundary of what one knows." It is so true: every new situation brings a fear with it, but because I now know it is coming, I get to choose whether or not to accept it. I choose not to because I want to grow and learn and that is also what I want for my children.

I have also, without being able to stop it, been the worst friend ever on many levels. Odd as it may seem, I actually feel no guilt about this as I know that I could not have done anything differently. The friendships that have survived are the ones that do not mind long periods of my being incommunicado. It is like radio silence. I am so busy looking for and researching all this information, then my mind is so busy understanding and learning it, then I am again so busy putting it into practise, everything that can possibly have a positive effect for the children and our family, that I have absolutely zero time left to "chat" to anyone. In fact, I cannot "chat" very well anymore at all. For most people, "chatting" is talking about what has happened in their lives - their car, their house, what their husband/wife, child, friend or family have done. All things that are over, have come and gone, are finished. I no longer have any interest in living in the past. I want to "chat" about the new information I have found that has an impact on how we will live our lives from here and on into the future. Things such as, that I never knew that when oncologists (cancer doctors) were asked, over 80% of them said that they would not do the treatments that they were recommending for their patients. Wow! Things such as, what I learnt in a documentary series called "The Quest for the Cure Continues" by Ty Bollinger *(www.thetruthaboutcancer.com)*, in which 28 doctors and 23 healthcare specialists discuss alternative therapies for treating cancer, and where you hear about patient after patient who is still alive, having lived up to 20 or more years cancer free after their diagnosis. Things such as, nutrition; if your immune system is strong your body can eliminate any sickness a lot of the time without us knowing we have it. So what foods are good for you? What foods boost and repair your immune system? What foods have anti-cancer properties? Things such as, where are the toxins coming from? Such as, where is the independent scientific proof for something? Or, why is the Standard American Diet called SAD? (By the way, it is not only the American diet but a lot of western diet in general). Or science, such as research on epigenomes, which shows that energy is controlling genes. Or that the atom, which was once thought to be the smallest molecule, is in fact itself full of energy that we cannot measure. I want to "chat" about health, homeopathy, yoga, new methods of heating your house, saunas, being self-reliant, and anything that improves people's well-being and lives.

Then friendships must be able to survive my "hard/bad days/times".

An example of this happened about two summers ago to some friends who came to stay with us on holiday in Connemara, a long standing yearly arrangement of several days duration. However, this particular year, for the couple of days before they arrived, I had been struggling with Cole's diabetes and the unfairness of the impact of it on his life, never being able to do things with complete spontaneity, always having to think about how his body was responding. The morning of our friend's arrival found me sitting by the water's edge in my togs, sobbing and wondering just how we were to cope for, well, forever. Of course, our friends did not know any of this, and so when they arrived bringing two unexpected but lovely small puppies along with themselves and their three children, they expected us to all to be delighted and not fazed in the slightest. Well, they were partly correct. The children were enchanted and Nicky did not appear to even notice, but I could not cope. I had nothing extra to give at the time. It just sort of tipped me from sitting on the edge of the abyss to hanging from the edge by my fingertips, my legs dangling off into the darkness. But the funny thing was how I responded. I did not feel anger as one might expect; I did not pull my hair out or fling my arms up in the air and scream or rant or push them into the water (friends and puppies!) I did and said nothing, nothing at all, because I felt nothing. It was as if I had gone completely numb inside and as if I was watching everything, myself included, from somewhere outside of my body. I was just observing. I watched myself talking to people, I responded to everyone, but it was distant and everyone felt it. To our friends, I am sure, I must have appeared to have transmogrified into the bitch from hell; but I could not help it and I did not care.

For days this went on; in fact, until they left with the puppies. Then slowly, it was as if my body was thawing out, I found that I was back on the edge of the abyss again with no idea how I had climbed back up there. I am quite sure that it was a coping mechanism, but unless you have been there it is not one that is easily understood. I wrote to our friends afterwards, way afterwards, at Christmas and tried to explain. While they were very nice about it, I knew that they did not get it. Sadly, I think that they probably do now, because they too have a child with challenges, and I suspect that recently one of them found themselves by the abyss or dangling over it. I truly wish that they still did not get it; I would not wish the experience on anyone.

Then there are the truly madcap things that I have done. Eight years ago, when I became 40, I happened to see a beautiful diamond solitaire ring in the window of an antiques shop and fell madly in love with it immediately. It called to me and I resolutely ignored it for weeks. After all, I had no money; we always seemed to be either barely ahead or living in the overdraft. So I told myself to stop being so ridiculous and to forget about the ring. But I could not. I longed for it, I dreamt about it; it annoyed the hell out of me. I told Nicky about it – probably in some vain hope that he would be able to magically produce the money from somewhere – where, for goodness sake? Behind his ears? In his socks? – and he too pointed out our lack of finances. But still I pined for the blasted thing. In the end, I decided that I must be having a midlife crisis! I thought about it (in fact, I did little else) and managed to come up with the justification that, as Nicky had never bought me a piece of jewellery (my engagement ring was my grandmother's, as that was what I wanted), and it was my 40th birthday, it would be perfectly reasonable for me to buy myself the ring! So I went to the Credit Union, and because I cannot lie, I told the lady exactly what I wanted to borrow the money for. She kindly said, "We'll just put down "home improvements", that's what everyone says", and gave me the loan. So I bought the ring and paid it off over the following year. I have never regretted it, silly and all as it seemed at the time. When I am having challenging days where I fail to see much beauty in the world, and am faced with facts such as, pharmaceutical companies are only out to make money (what else did I expect? They are businesses whose bottom line is to make a profit for their shareholders; they care more about sales than safety); or that even though doctors are obviously clever people, the majority seem not to be able to think outside the box and believe unquestioningly what the pharmaceutical companies tell them, I look at my ring, which is permanently on my finger, and it shines back at me like my own personal rainbow and reminds me of beautiful things.

There is one other thing, an emotional thing, that I feel compelled to share with you, and I am so glad that you are not standing in front of me right now, because it is so hard to say and I would have to look at the ground or over your shoulder or just close my eyes in order to say this at all, if you were present. Remember I told you, way back at the beginning of our story that relationships only worked if both sides were willing and able to put the work into them? Well, I told you that I was so tired that I could not, and this is true, but there is more, so much more. After Cole was diagnosed with T1, Nicky and I were barely surviving - we rarely saw each other, we were like ships passing in the night and I was living on fumes and sheer will power. Well, it would have been so much easier if we could have been intimate, if we could have even been physically close for just the briefest of times, but it was me who could not. I tried, because I so desperately wanted to loose myself in the moment, to find that wonderful release of, well everything. But if I did, this incredibly overpowering guilt would come crashing down on me afterwards. I would be overcome with guilt that I had forgotten, even for the briefest of times, about Cole's diabetes, because he could not, nor would he ever be able to. No matter what he does in life, he will always have to be aware of what his bloods are doing; if he chooses to ignore them and wing it he runs the risk of crashing and burning afterwards. Parents of children with T1 must be the only ones who are actually happy when their child is sharing their bed with someone else, because then we know that there is someone there with them, where we cannot be, listening to their breathing, being aware of their body movements - too much (having a fit) or too little (unconscious) - and able to respond and help them if they need it. I could not live with this guilt and so grew a little more distant and the gulf between Nicky and I grew even wider. Nicky had no idea how to reach me and bring me back. Nor did I.

It was not until I heard an incredibly brave colleague talk about the death of his child that I understood that I was grieving. He described exactly how I felt, but of course in his case it was because his child was dead and would never be able to experience any of the things that he himself was still able to, ever again. He described how he felt, "What right do I have to be happy when he cannot?" which I realised was what I was feeling. Of course, I totally realise that Cole is alive, and rationally I know that he is happy a lot of the time but what I realised that day was that I was grieving for the life that he had lost, the one that every parent expects for their child. We all expect them to be healthy and to tear through life with the totally unshakeable belief of youth that they are indestructible. I realised that this was what he would never do, that he would constantly be keeping himself alive and healthy, with no breaks, for the rest of his life.

I cannot begin to thank this person for sharing their experiences, because once I realised that I was grieving for the expected lost life, I could allow myself to do just that, grieve, and so start to heal, and also make a vow: that while Cole may always have to be, every day for the rest of his life, consciously keeping himself alive and healthy, I will do everything within my power to make sure that he can still do and achieve anything he wishes to. That is my job; to make sure that he realises that diabetes is just a part of him, it does not define him; he defines it. Consequently, I will not allow anyone to call him a diabetic, because that would allow diabetes to define him. Never happening, not ever, not on my watch.

# Chapter 20

So back to our story. At this time, Théa was going into fifth year in school, Ariana into third and Cole was starting into first year of secondary school. I am not sure that I have the words to explain to you how hard it was to let Cole go to boarding school. I found it hard to let all my children go. I would much rather have kept them with me for as long as possible, but they wished to go, having heard from their father how much he enjoyed it. And looking back now, I know that it was the right decision, as both Théa and Cole adored the social side of boarding and have formed some amazing friendships. While Ariana did not enjoy the social side that was to do with her Asperger's and not the school, and she would never have endured in the rigidity of the local schools. In fact, I am quite sure that she could only have survived in either a Steiner or Quaker school, with their accepting and valuing of each child's individuality. Anyway, while I had found it hard to let Ariana go to boarding school as I had no idea how she would survive without me to interpret life for her. Or if she would walk out the gate into the world with all its dangers or end it all because it got too much for her. I was terrified to let Cole go because just one simple miss calculation with his insulin could cause him to end up unconscious in a coma, and at least three hours away from me. But as I have said, both Nicky and I have always striven to bring up our children to be independent and think for themselves; we have always told them that they are never to take anything we say as gospel, they are always free to question it and decide what course their lives should follow, as long as they follow one simple rule: they must always act out of love - love for themselves first, and then humanity. Cole wanted to go to boarding school, so there was never any question that I would stop him, no matter what it cost me emotionally, and it did.

Almost everyone outside of our immediate family, the five of us, automatically assumed that as Cole was now away from home my life was easier, as I did not have to do all the calculations for his insulin requirements and carbohydrate count for him. I am not sure who they thought was doing my part for him. Or maybe they thought that a 12-year-old boy was suddenly capable of doing it all for himself overnight, without ever making a mistake. Certainly, I had made quite a few spectacular bloomers over the previous four years and spent several hours rectifying them, trying to keep him conscious and out of hospital, so why on earth would it be safe to assume he would not too. While his pump did a lot of the calculations for him, it could not automatically adjust his insulin requirements for him, for example if he was doing sports. Nor was there anyone there to remind him to check his bloods regularly or, and this was a particularly terrifying prospect, to remind him to bring his bag with his meter, spare "parts" (sets/needles, insulin, reservoirs) and things to treat "lows" (medical glucagon, a last resort and has to be given by a bystander, as if needed Cole will be unconscious; and some form of fast-acting sugar such as Coke) with him if he left the school grounds on a day trip, such as to play an away match.

When Cole started school Nicky and I went in and talked to all the teachers. We gave a very brief description of how to help Cole keep safe – it is impossible to impart in half an hour or so, anything but the briefest of overviews. It is like trying to tell a person who has always driven an automatic car how to drive a manual car in half an hour - impossible. We both knew that they did not get it and that it would be impossible for them not to mash the gears. We just had to hope that they would be responsible enough to ask us to help them learn without stripping the gears. In other words, that they would call us and ask us what to do when they found themselves concerned about Cole, so that he did not end up in hospital because they had not asked for help. One thing that was readily agreed by all the teachers, was that Cole's mobile phone would be viewed as if it was a piece of medical equipment and that he was allowed to call me at any time, day or night, if he needed my advice. They agreed that even if he were to abuse this, his phone was never to be taken from him. They could give him a detention or restrict his privileges, but never were they to take his phone or stop him from calling me or Nicky.

So Cole went off to school. We agreed that he would call me every morning and night to tell me how he was managing and what his bloods were doing. We also agreed that he would not eat after tea so that he had no extra active insulin in his body when he was going to sleep. This was so important to me because, even though his CGM (continuous glucose monitor) talked to his pump and the pump would suspend delivery of his background insulin if it said that he was a certain low reading, the sensors for the CGM could go off track. In the beginning I did not know why, nor it seemed did any of the medical profession. So I did not want any extra insulin driving his bloods lower and lower, especially if he had done sports that day, as it was quite possible for him to experience a low anything up to 16 hours or so after being active. In fact, there have been many nights where the CGM has suspended the pump for the whole night (it rechecks every two hours) and Cole has woken the next morning, having had no background insulin all night, with his bloods being between 4 and 6mmols, which is perfect. I try not to think what would have happened if the pump had not suspended but continued to deliver insulin, because the reality of it is that he would have had extremely low blood glucose readings all night and who knows if he would have woken in the morning, or been in a coma, or worse, dead. That is our reality and the reality of every family with a T1 child, though we always choose to be proactive rather than reactive, to avoid this situation ever happening.

Often our pro-activeness is interpreted by outsiders as controlling, and oddly, we have found that on multiple occasions, for some reason best known to themselves, people have felt the need to share with us their unasked for opinions on our parenting styles and how they think we should do things. This is made even odder by the fact that those who share their views with us never have children with challenges and so are blissfully unaware of what our lives are like 24/7. Lucky them. There have been many nights where Cole and I have been awake till midnight or later, sorting out lows or highs; or where he has called me in the middle of the night because he has woken either by himself because he felt "odd", or by a friend who has been woken by the pump alarming, and given him a poke or thrown something at him to wake him so he can shut the alarm up. One of the hardest things to do is to keep him awake for an hour or more while he is low, over the phone, till his bloods are at a constant level when I can make a broad assumption that he might be alright till the morning. We talk about things we love, like holidays in Connemara, Christmas with my parents, our family, his friends, inventions that he would like to make or has made, magic; the list is long because an hour or more, when your child is already tired and his low is making him groggy, is an awfully long and frightening time in the dark of night when everyone else is asleep and we seem to be alone in the world.

When Cole went to school, Théa and Ariana both slept with their phones close by and switched on in case I could not keep Cole awake and could not raise the dorm master. While I have had to wake the dorm master in the middle of the night because Cole was not answering me anymore, had gone silent and not answered his phone even when I re-rang it again and again many times, I have not had to call the girls. On that occasion the dorm master had been able to rouse Cole, who on checking his bloods, had been fine. He had just been exhausted due to lack of sleep; and because lows always make him tired too. He had been able to go back to sleep that night, but

I'll tell you this for nothing: that night I was not sure if I would ever be able to sleep again. One of the hardest things for the two of us is that the next day everyone expects us to be firing on all four cylinders and to be full of the joys of life like we always are, because they have absolutely no idea that we are functioning with sleep deprivation, or that lows have a physical and mental effect on Cole for many hours afterwards. His capacity to recall information or problem-solve is not as lightning fast as normal.

So Cole called me every night and again every morning, because I wanted to know, and still do, that he is alive and has woken up to a new and glorious-to-be-alive day! Cole is now in fifth year, and at 17, wishes to have more independence, quite understandably, so he still calls me before bed and now gives me a text in the morning. Well, that is the theory. Usually, in the morning I send him a text after not hearing from him, and he responds. I get texts like, "Alive no need to worry", I would love more information but at least I know the salient point, that he is alive. At night I call him again because he is far too busy to think of calling his mum. He is a typical teenage boy, so at times, all his brain cells appear to have gone into hibernation and rarely engage together! In fact, I am sure that I can hear grinding noises when they do. He also seems to have lost the ability to communicate with me, though I notice with interest that this is not the case with his friends. His speech appears to be quite normal and adequate when he is talking with them. However, all I get are grunts and shoulder shrugs with the occasional monosyllabic word thrown in when he notices that I look as if I am about to explode! This is all as it should be, no different from his peers, and yet it is so much more and has the potential to come between us even more than it would his peers and their parents. You see, Cole cannot afford to let this teenage "Oh my parents are such control freaks", "My parents are such nags", and "My parents have no idea how to have fun" phase affect his control on his diabetes. He cannot take a few years off with his peers to bum around with a devil-may-care attitude, and think of nothing but his own satisfaction before they all decide to re-enter this world and be part of humanity again, because if he does, he will probably either end up in hospital now a few times or cause such damage to his body that he will suffer for it in the near future, and shorten his lifespan considerably.

So I am again dancing on a tightrope, trying to keep him answering my texts and phone calls, constantly thinking of how best to say things so that there is a hope he will take it on board, and always holding an image of him in my mind where he is happy and laughing and safe. Because, as he so rightly points out to me, how am I going to "make" him do anything now? He is taller and broader than me, can physically lift me up and place me out of his way when I stand in front of him; and when he wants to, can easily reason and put forward a very objective, rational and intelligent argument to any objection that I can come up with. So I see myself a little like Jiminy Cricket in Pinocchio; I am not his conscience, but that little nagging voice inside his head that is constantly reminding him of all that he needs to do every day in relation to T1 to stay alive and safe until after I have gone, because that is how it should be. I should grow old and die before him, with him being healthy and strong, and that is what I strive for. So, as in the movie, I am sometimes running madly along after him, in reality as well as figuratively inside his head, calling out to him to remember this or that, while he is charging off into his wonderful life. Boy, do my legs feel short and tired sometimes, and my voice a little croaky!

At the moment Cole is rebelling against life itself. I can understand this, really I can. I hated life at 17, his current age - everything seemed so unfair. I felt like I had every right to be treated like an adult, and in some ways I was; everyone from my parents to teachers expected me to toe the line and act responsibly when it came to study, part-time jobs and helping out out home. Yet while I was expected to act like an adult, I felt I was never given the respect of being consulted about any of the decisions concerning the direction my life was taking. So I try very hard to talk to Cole about everything that is going on for him.

"Cole, are your checking your bloods at least three times a day? Because you know my preference would be for a minimum of four times a day, when you wake, lunch time, dinner time and bed time, don't you?"

"No and yes"

"So no, you are not checking three times a day?"

"Yes"

Breathe, big, deep, calming breaths. Out of the side of my eye I watch him, knowing he is watching me, waiting to see how I will deal with this piece of information. If I fail the test and react like an exploding rocket, he will switch off and not answer my future questions, because as he puts it, "what's the point in telling you things that are just going to upset you?"

A little light bulb blinks on inside my head and I ask, "Cole, do you even carry your meter around with you during the day?"

"No."

More deep, slow, supposedly calming breaths, (they lie, they are not calming, they just give you time to think!). "So what happens if you want to eat at lunch time? How do you check your bloods so that you can work out how much insulin to give? Or are you just winging it?"

"I only eat meat, no carbs" (protein technically needs no insulin).

"Hmm. Not ideal really. What if you were high or low? You would not know until there was a problem and you know that sometimes if you eat very few carbs for a long while, your body will treat some of the protein as if it were carbs and need some insulin?"

"Yes, I know"

"So do you think you could start doing your bloods before eating anything?"

"Maybe." In other words, no, I am just saying this to get you off of my case.

"If you did do your bloods when you were supposed to or wore your CGM (something he has stopped doing), I wouldn't have to repeat myself so often. Contrary to what you think, I do not wake up in the morning and go, 'Oh good another day where I get to nag Cole and be on his case the whole time; my very favourite pastime'!"

A harrumphing sort of half laugh escapes him at this, because we both know that that is exactly what he thinks, that my sole ambition and purpose in life, at the moment, is to be a right pain in the butt to him.

At the moment his school work is, well, a nice word for it would be struggling, a more truthful word would be abysmal. His Christmas report had a glowing description from his house master as to what a well-balanced, pleasant and easy going young man he is, and how he is a pleasure to have in the boarding house, just what every parent wishes to hear; but his subject marks showed that he was just about turning up for class and the exams, but not in any way straining himself, perhaps putting pen to paper long enough to write down his name and the first few things that came into his head. I read his report and thought about things for a while. Then I came to a decision that I ran by Nicky and he agreed. I talked with Cole and told him, "You know what your subject results are like and why they are so. I am not going to be on your case about your school work. Dad and I are much more concerned about your passive rebellion as regards to managing your diabetes. If I am constantly on at you about managing your bloods and your school work, I think that you will give up talking to me altogether and I will lose you. You will completely rebel and I do not want that to happen. I am much more concerned about getting you through this rebellion with your limbs still attached to your body, your eyesight still 20/20 and your body still in as near to perfect condition as possible, thus avoiding any health complications down the line."

"I'm not rebelling, I'm just a bit lazy."

"Cole, just because you are not completely derailing, doing drugs, drinking and smoking does not mean that you are not rebelling. Your 'laziness' is a form of passive rebellion, and I can completely understand that. I can only imagine what a pain in the butt it must be to always have to check your bloods before eating, or doing sports, or walking down town, or just anything, as well as adjusting your insulin requirements several times a day, every day. I get that talking to me twice a day is a total intrusion and one that your friends do not have put up with. So I can understand your 'laziness', but I just cannot stand by and let it happen, because I am afraid of the consequences. So I am choosing my battles. I am choosing to nag you and remind you about all that you need to do regarding your health and staying alive. Because I have a plan: I am going to live to be 90 or older; and in this plan you are going to be alive and healthy too so that I can still be bugging the hell out of you. (This gets a smile out of him.) Your school work is your choice, you can always go back to college as a mature student, and anyway you already think that you would like to do something more hands on like blacksmithing. I just want you to be happy and healthy and alive. Though this is not a free for all, I am not offering to support you for the rest of your life", (this too draws out a smile).

Shortly after this "talk", and I use the term lightly because mostly it was just me doing the talking, I have my decision validated. I meet someone whom I have not talked to for a very long time, life just got busy, you know, and when I tell her this story in answer to her question about how Cole is doing she says, "You know, you're right"

This strikes me as odd because she was a teacher for a very long time, and loved to impart knowledge and help her students to grow and learn, so I am a bit surprised and it must have shown on my face, because she started to explain without me saying anything.

"I know of this child, who has had type 1 diabetes for several years now but has never really been able to get a handle on things. Now this child is blind, and waiting for a transplant."

Wow! Now, as you know, I usually hate it when people tell me horror stories related to diabetes, but not today. Today I am so very sad for this child and the family and I wish them all the best, but I also know, without a shadow of a doubt, that I am right in my decision to be on Cole's case about his diabetes only, and not his school work. I cannot afford to cloud the issue with school work and risk losing all communication with him. To do so would be to put his health and life at risk, and I will not do that. So I go home and I tell Nicky, and we hug each other and feel for those other parents, and we thank the universe that we have an opportunity here to reach out and help Cole. Then I tell Cole, so that he can see that I am not just making these things up, though of course he knows I am not. But sometimes we need to hear about something close to home just for a reality check, and then we move on, back to our positive lives.

# Chapter 21

All the while this was going on I was also still helping Ariana, who while improving continually on the detox, would still need my help to sort out some social situations. On average, this would be two or three times a week, and when they did happen, it was usually spectacularly upsetting for her. An example of one would be that the new dorm mistress seemed to be unable to make any allowances for the family situations of the girls in Ariana's year. So when one girl was having a particularly hard time adjusting to her mother having a boyfriend, the first since her parents' divorce, the dorm mistress would cut her no slack at all. If she was late, or guilty of any minor misdemeanour, she was still berated and not given the love and support she needed. Ariana found this particularly hard to comprehend and allow because, after all, they were in a Quaker school whose ethos was to love, accept and help everyone. So she would get completely wound up over the unfairness of the situation. This is where my diplomatic skills came to the fore. I would listen to Ariana, and when she had said all that she had to on the subject, I would agree that I also found the dorm mistress' attitude less than loving and then ask what she thought she might be going to do about it.

"Tell her she is completely uncaring, horrid and mean. That this is a Quaker school and that it is supposed to be loving and accepting of all people. That if someone has done something that she does not like, she should be able to talk to them about it and explain why it is not acceptable, and give them the opportunity to behave better, not yell and rant at them. You always said that yelling at someone was unacceptable!"

She was correct of course, because Ariana always remembers everything verbatim. I do think that yelling is an unacceptable form of communication, especially with children. Children learn and grow when you take time to explain things to them, and why it might be inappropriate to do or say something. I have never seen a child who is yelled at, grow. They certainly learn something: to yell when things do not go their way and that it is alright to make someone else feel small, inadequate and unloved. Part of me was tempted to just let her off. However, I did not want that women yelling at my already fragile child, so we came up with a compromise. Together, Ariana and I compiled a list of the dorm mistress' behaviour that we felt was inappropriate and why, and I wrote to the school. While in the long term my letter, and those of other parents who were dissatisfied with the mistress' behaviour, had the desired effect in that a new mistress was appointed, it was too slow to be of any benefit for Ariana.

She soldiered on through third year and really did extremely well compared to the previous two years, but we, Nicky, Ariana and I, decided that she would not do her state exams at the end of the year. Part of the reason for this was that the questions in exam papers are always ambiguous to Ariana. She reads the question and answers it directly. She does not "fill out" the answer with extra relevant information, which the examiner and teachers assume that the child will do, because the question did not ask directly for it. Ariana knows all the information; she is very bright, but she is also very literal. She will give you exactly what you asked for and assume that if you did not ask for something you did not want it. Also, where, if she were to start to "fill out" the answer, is she supposed to stop? Because one can always link more and more to a topic. The other reason was that the teachers had less time to explain to Ariana what they wanted from her. I explained that this was probably because, unlike Nicky and I, some parents felt that it was the teacher's job, and some teachers felt this too, to push and drive the children to achieve more. Again, this was something foreign to Ariana as I have always maintained that if a child is happy and encouraged they will achieve more than if they are reprimanded. Théa and her friends are a wonderful example of this; they have all always loved to learn and achieve more for themselves, without being pushed by anyone, and they are very successful at what they do.

Fourth year in the children's school is called Transition Year. In this year they do minimal school subjects while spending a lot of time doing activities that broaden the children's minds; exposing them to the world outside and helping them mature. They work within the local community helping those less fortunate or younger or older than them; they participate in outdoor pursuits that require them to both learn new activities such as kayaking and rock climbing, and to work together in groups to make sure that all of them reach the final destination together. Both Théa and Cole adored it and they came out the other end far more mature, with a broader outlook on life, and having had a lot of fun in the process.

However, at the end of Ariana's third year, we decided as a family that it would not suit Ariana, or be a pleasant experience for her or us. We had several reasons for this. Firstly, each new activity would involve a different group of her peers, thus entailing a whole new social interaction, with her trying to learn and understand what made each individual "tick" (happy, sad, mad etc.). Each activity had a different goal, set of rules, expectations and organiser. Several of the activities required interacting with people outside of the school, whom Ariana had not met before. Most adults do not afford teenagers the same respect that they would another adult, and Ariana can see no logic in this, as they expect the teenager to conform to adult rules and expectations, give them the same responsibility as adults, but also expect to be able to dictate to them in a manner that they would not use with another adult. Secondly, Théa was going into her final year in school, at the end of which she would sit her state exams that would determine if she got into college or not. We all felt, Ariana included, that if Ariana was constantly in a state of agitation because of the frequent group/rule changes, she would be upset, would not enjoy any of the activities and would need a lot more help and time, and that this would make it very much harder for Théa to study in a peaceful and conducive environment. Thirdly, by this time, Ariana had had enough of dealing with the current dorm mistress.

So we took Ariana out of school for the year. She stayed at home and did several activities for the year from home. She attended a Makeup School in a city an hour away from us, and did two courses concurrently during the year: one a diploma course and the other the foundation year of the higher diploma. This was an amazing achievement for her and we were so proud of her. On the first day at the school, she walked off into a completely alien environment, full of people she had not met by herself, and managed to survive and even enjoy some of it! It turned out that, actually, Ariana functioned very well in a third level education system; mostly because all the people on the course had chosen to be there and so were happy to learn the subject being taught. They were all mature and so there was none of the sniping or volatility that there can be with teenagers, and, best of all, Ariana found that she had a flare for makeup and a special interest in special effects makeup. Also, during that year, she took up learning Spanish.

At the end of the year she did return to school, entering fifth year. However, after half the year, she, Nicky and I decided that it just was not for her. While she actually liked being back with her peers, and now had an achievement under her belt – the diploma in makeup and the special effects makeup- which gave her much more confidence in herself when she was in group situations, she was unhappy still with the attitude of the dorm mistress and the set-up in dorms. Just before the end of the Christmas term, we went as a family to my parents for an annual weekend excursion to the pantomime with all the cousins, followed by a family dinner. It was a great weekend and Ariana managed all the social interaction wonderfully. However, on the Monday morning, the day of returning to school, she came to me in the morning and said, "Mum, I woke up this morning crying. That has not happened for over a year now."

"Do you know why?"

"I think it is because of being back at school."

"Do you want to go back today?"

"Yes, because I do not want to quit or let you and Dad down."

I explained that she could never let me or Nicky down and must not ever continue with something just for that reason. We loved her and just wanted her to be happy. She must only continue with something if she wanted to. She said that she did want to keep trying and would return to school that day. On the journey back to school, Ariana fell asleep in the car and after about half an hour, what I can only describe as a guttural cry tore out of her body. I woke her up and asked her if she was alright to which she answered, no. To me she looked and sounded just like the child of three years previous.

"Ariana, I do not think you should go back to school. You have come so far, and now all I see is you slipping back; it's not worth it. I do not want to go back there, none of us do. I do not think any of us could survive going through all that again."

"I do not want to go back there either, but I do not want to be a failure, someone who gives up", said a small and frightened voice.

"I think that you are an amazing person. Do you remember what the psychologist who diagnosed your Asperger's said? He said that he was absolutely amazed that you could even attend a boarding school and that you functioned incredibly well in society; and you have come even further since then. So you are not a failure or a giver-upper; you are an incredibly brave young woman of whom your father and I are very proud of."

I then asked Cole, who was with us in the car, was he happy to return to school that day on his own, as it would be the first time he would be there without either of his sisters, Théa having now gone to college. Part of me wanted him to say no, as I was not sure that I was ready for him to be there on his own! But he said he was, and another part of me was delighted that he was so happy and confident there. I called Nicky, explained what had happened, and before I even said what we were doing he said, "Bring her home, we are not doing that to her." See why I love that man? He may be completely absorbed in his own world most of the time, not notice when I dye my hair pink (true!), but when the going gets tough, he always backs me up.

So Ariana came home and Cole went to school on his own, and another chapter in our lives began.

# Chapter 22

Cole was very happy at school and Ariana was much happier out of it. We found other learning experiences for Ariana. She loved, and was good at, special effects make up, so we found courses run by professional bodies in Ireland and abroad for her to do, and she managed them beautifully, dealing with the stress of new social situations and people with ever increasing skill. When attending courses that were in Ireland, she would even manage to stay alone in a bed and breakfast during the week, something that I would never have imagined possible just a couple of years earlier. For the ones abroad, I would travel with her, as we did not feel that she needed to be put under that stress yet; and anyway she was barely 17 by then. She loved them and learnt a variety of things such as body painting, which is when you use the human body as a canvas and either paint it with a theme to make it stand out or blend into the background; how to use different mediums like latex to build a totally different face like that of a werewolf or a witch or make gruesome flesh wounds; as well as how to apply make up to make one look stunning.

Whenever I had spare time, I continued my learning. I have spent the last 15 years looking at and learning all I can about "health" so that I could improve our lives and, hopefully, those of others. I have actively sought out information that came from medically trained doctors who have questioned the information that they have been taught, because this makes sense to me as it looks at both sides. During this time, I have studied our current medical system very carefully, in the beginning not through choice, but because I had to, as it was failing my children. I had been brought up to believe that doctors were good people who worked within a medical system whose sole purpose was the "health" of the patient. What I have learnt over the years is that this would appear to be a fallacy. Of course, there are some good doctors who genuinely care about their patients and who question where their information comes from, its truthfulness and its value to the patient, but there are many more who do not question anything.

Doctors, by default, must be academically clever people to obtain the high qualifications necessary to enter medical school. They study and learn the anatomy and physiology of the human body and the diseases that affect it, which is incredibly detailed and requires a good degree of intelligence to understand and recall. Then they learn about all the drugs that there are to "treat" the diseases of the human body, and the vaccines that there are to prevent some of these diseases. What strikes me as odd is that no time at all is spent on how to prevent diseases in the first place, except by vaccine. They do not look into nutrition in depth, nor the impact of lifestyle on the body. They accept without questioning during their training, that vaccines were the sole reason that people stopped dying from all the diseases for which vaccines are available, even though they never see any independent science to back this up. Yet they also accept that diseases for which there are no vaccines, such as cholera, rheumatic fever, scarlet fever, typhoid and typhus, declined because of better sanitation and nutrition. In general, they do not think it odd that they are being told that better social and nutritional conditions only had an effect on some diseases and not all.

This becomes even stranger when you consider that modern medicine considers Hippocrates to be its "father" and he said the following:

*"Let food be thy medicine and medicine be thy food."*

Yet nutrition is barely mentioned in medical school. In fact, it would appear that what is really taught in medical school is how to "manage" disease, not how to prevent or reverse it. It is funny, but I had always assumed that the medical profession wanted us to be "healthy". However, when I actually thought about this, it occurred to me that if we were all healthy there would be a lot of doctors and people in the pharmaceutical industry who would be out of a job.

The more I dealt with the medical profession as a whole, the less I liked what I saw. I have always thought, and still do, that the medical profession shines and is second to none when it comes to treating trauma. They do amazing things in this area, and without question save many, many lives. However, they seem to be failing abysmally when it comes to maintaining long term health. I have never, ever heard anyone in the medical profession say, "Let's look for the cause of the cancer", or indeed ask, "What is causing the massive increase in autism, type 1 diabetes, MS etc.?" They, and the pharmaceutical industries, are always looking for "the cure", but never "the cause". It makes one wonder why. Surely it would be better for people never to get these diseases in the first place? To address the cause of a person's disease, to help their body heal itself and to teach them how to stay healthy, is surely the highest and purest of ideals. The conclusion that I have come to, is that currently the medical profession believe that it is not possible for the body to heal itself, that we were created to a flawed design, and that our environment, the food we eat and the toxins we allow into our body, have absolutely no effect on our health - a belief that is encouraged by the pharmaceutical industry. Odd, considering Hippocrates previous statement and his following one:

*"Natural forces within us are the true healers of disease."*

To me it would make sense for doctors to get their information from independent studies, but this is not the case. Doctors get their information on drugs directly from the pharmaceutical companies or from peer-reviewed journals. So let's take a closer look at both these sources. A great book on how pharmaceutical companies work, and the relationships between them and the healthcare industry, doctors and medical journals, is a book written by Peter C Gøtzsche, who is a physician, a scientist and a researcher. The book is called *Deadly Medicines and Organised Crime – How big pharma has corrupted healthcare*. It will challenge all that you thought you knew. Though I suspect by this stage you are already realising that what we have been led to believe by those in charge of "health" is not always true. A lot of the following information can be found in this book and also on the internet, and will be eye opening to those of you who may not have thought about it before.

In his book, Mr Gøtzsche tells how pharmaceutical companies are repeatedly found guilty of corporate crimes and gives many examples. They are fined millions, and even billions, of dollars again and again, but this does not stop them from repeating offences which kill and harm many people. To them it is just the cost of business; the fines are miniscule compared to the amounts that they make on the sales of drugs. To you and me, though, it is a potential life sentence of pain and misery, or death. In fact, in the US in 2013, the pharmaceutical industry paid almost $3.75 billion to the government in criminal and civil fines. All one has to do is put "pharmaceutical industry and fines" into a search engine; and masses of evidence will appear as to how corrupt and fraudulent the industry is.

Peter Gøtzsche also explains how clinical trials, that are the "gold standard" by which all drugs are compared, are very often flawed. We have always been told that trials are 'blinded': that is that the people taking part in them, and those administering the drugs and placebos, do not know who is being given what, placebo or drug. However, apparently, often the prescriber does know who is being given the drug and who the placebo because the pills look different. Also, the patient can know too, if they have taken the drug before, as it may look different or they may know that when they took the drug previously, they experienced side effects such as a dry mouth.

Science can only be proven if an experiment can be replicated again and again with the same result by any scientist. Drugs trials do not do this. They are not replicated by many different scientists who are not funded directly or indirectly by the drug companies. Another factor with the drugs that we are told are safe is that the information that we receive, is not always the same as the information that the drugs regulatory agencies receive.

In fact, the information that doctors receive from journals and drug companies is also often not the same as the information that the drug regulatory agencies received. Why not?

In Europe and the United States prescribed drugs are known to be the third leading cause of death, coming only after heart disease and cancer. I would suggest that prescribed drugs actually might be higher on the list, because many cancer patients take chemotherapy which is completely toxic and has a listed side effect of being carcinogenic (causing cancer), so if they die, did they die of their original cancer or a secondary cancer caused by their drugs or by toxic poisoning? Also, many people who die of heart disease are actually on prescribed drugs. When they die does anyone check what drugs they were on and was heart disease a listed side effect?

Now let's see where we are with this. Drug companies fund most of the trials on their own drugs, own the data from these trials and decide what data to make public to the regulatory agencies, the doctors and the public.

So how do the doctors get there information about drugs? They read peer-reviewed journals, such as *Lancet, BMJ (British Medical Journal)* and *New England Journal of Medicine.* These journals publish papers on new drugs and research which are published under the name of a doctor. A lot of these doctors are in fact approached by the drugs company once the paper has already been written by a 'ghost writer', employed by the company conducting or funding the trial, and they are offered a large amount of money to put their name to the paper. Often they do not read the research at all, only the abstract which can be misleading, not listing any of the adverse side effects associated with the drug.

Frighteningly, a search on the internet will bring you to many former editors of medical journals who are all, based on their years of experience, saying the same thing: that pharmaceutical companies are pulling the strings when it comes to the information that doctors are getting about drugs. The following were all freely found on the internet.

A former editor of the *Lancet*, Richard Horton has stated:

> *"Journals have devolved into information laundering operations for the pharmaceutical industry."* (Horton, 2004)

Dr Marcia Angell, former editor of the *New England Journal of Medicine* has said that:

> *"It is simply no longer possible to believe much of the clinical research that is published, or to rely on the judgement of trusted physicians or authoritative medical guidelines. I take no pleasure in this conclusion, which I reached slowly and reluctantly over my two decades as an editor of The New England Journal of Medicine."* (Angell, 2009) *(http://www. nybooks.com/articles/archives/2009/jan/15/drug-companies-doctorsa-story-of-corruption/)*

Dr Jerome Kassirer, another former editor of *The New England Journal of Medicine* has said:

> *"The industry has deflected the moral compasses of many physicians."* (Kassirer, 2004)

Other doctors get there information from attending talks given by their colleagues, whom they, of course, trust. Yet the majority of these colleagues are paid thousands of pounds/dollars by drug companies to give these talks. Some even get paid so much for giving talks that they have agents to negotiate their fees. It is highly unlikely, that if they were to speak out about any side effects, that they would ever be employed again, so their information is just what the pharmaceutical company employing those wants the doctors to hear.

Thus it would seem that all the information on which your doctor is basing his decision, as to which drug to prescribe to you for your ailment, is biased.

The current medical system would seem to have decided that a baby is born with a deficient immune system; that we were created flawed. Kind of odd, considering that the human species has survived for more than a million years. If our immune system was so flawed, we would have died out long ago. With this assumption, that our immune system is unable to keep us alive, they often start to give babies antibiotics at birth, "just in case", or "to prevent" something. Antibiotics are completely indiscriminate and kill all gut bacteria, good and bad, not just ones that cause disease. So often we have a new born baby with a seriously impaired gut flora - remember that we already know that 80% of our immune system is within our gut. So it makes sense that this baby, with a now impaired immune system because of antibiotics, will have to struggle to maintain optimum health and is wide open to any opportunistic bacteria or virus that comes its way; it was not born this way but made this way by medical intervention. Then, within a very short period of time, the medical profession begin to inject toxins into this tiny little human body in the form of vaccines. So now this tiny little human body is trying to deal with toxins that have bypassed 80% of its immune system, toxins that its body would never have had to deal with under normal circumstances, and which are in quantities that are considered dangerous for an adult to ingest. How can this even begin to make any sense to anyone? Certainly it does not to me, and I cannot understand where my logical brain was when I allowed this to happen to my precious babies. What was I thinking? The truth was that I was not thinking at all. I was acting out of fear and a misplaced trust.

If I was given the opportunity over again, would I vaccinate? No. Because I have done my research now. Based on 1960 figures, prior to the measles vaccine being introduced, my child had a 1 in 10,000 chance of dying from measles.(Halvorsen, 2007) Today my child has a 1 in 80 to a 1 in 50 chance of being autistic; and we are finding out that vaccines are linked to causing autism, so I would take my chances with the measles virus, because I also know that children who have good nutrition and whose immune system is strong are far less likely to suffer any ill effects from the measles .

The World Health Organisation (WHO) reports that in the year 2000 there were 3,000 deaths world wide from diphteria. *(http://www.who.int/immunization/topics/diphtheria/en/index1.html)* Given that the current world population is 7.2 billion, that means that the risk of dying from diphtheria today is approximately 0.0004 in 1,000 or 1 in 2,500,000. In 2008, the WHO reports, there were 89,000 deaths worldwide from whooping cough (pertussis). *(http://www.who.int/immunization/monitoring_surveillance/burden/vpd/surveillance_type/passive/pertussis/en/)* So approximately a 0.124 in 1,000 or 1 in 8,065 chance of dying from whooping cough. The DPT vaccine is being linked with the following diseases/deaths: Type 1 diabetes which a child has a 1 in 4,167 chance of getting, cot deaths *(http://www.whale.to/vaccines/cot_death.html)* where the chances are 2 in 1,000 (or 1 in 500) or more likely 7-10 in 1,000. (Scheibner, 1993) Again, based on my findings, I would rather boost my child's immune system, nutrition and health and if they were to catch a disease, to treat it appropriately with either homeopathy, or if required, medical intervention.

All my research has convinced me that the risks from vaccines to my children far outweigh the risks from catching the disease.

For example, some of the adverse effects, or side effects, currently listed by Merck for its MMR vaccine are: atypical measles, parotitis (which, when infectious, is mumps), inflammation disorders of the skin and cardiovascular (heart) system, diabetes mellitus (type 1), disorders of the blood, anaphylaxis (life threatening allergic reaction), oedema (swelling), arthritis, myalgia (muscle pain), encephalitis (swelling of the brain), meningitis, pneumonia, nerve deafness and death. *(http:// www.merck.com/product/usa/pi_circulars/m/mmr_ii/mmr_ii_pi.pdf)*

Hippocrates said, *"As to diseases, make a habit of two things, to help or at least do no harm."*

Are we really helping with vaccines, or are we doing harm?

For myself and Nicky, we believe that we did more harm than good to our children. We have all had to live daily - and daily is 24 hours, not just the ones we are supposed to be awake for - with the consequences of our actions, i.e. not informing ourselves before making those decisions. There is no history of auto-immune disease, type 1 diabetes, or autism, on either side of the family. The following is an example of the results of our uninformed actions.

The summer after Cole got his pump, we went on our holidays to the wilds of Connemara; no phone, no electricity and no Nicky in the beginning as he was abroad on business. During Nicky's absence, we managed to flood Cole's pump with salt water. The waterproof bag in which it was housed, though very durable and thick, got a tiny nick in it and I did not notice. I was new to all this and for some reason it never occurred to me to check the integrity of the bag each evening after use. One morning, while we were playing on the beach, Cole said, "Mum, there's water in the pump bag."

I looked in horror at the bag, emptied it and looked at the pump - no readings on the screen, just completely blank - it had obviously been wet for a while. I dried it, took the battery out and put a new battery in. Nothing. I was sick to the stomach and Cole was deathly white, apologising for having made a hole in the bag. We could not even see one, it was that small, but nothing I could say would convince him that he could not have done anything to avoid it. Cole and I sat into the car, as it was the only place with reception, to use the mobile phone to call the pump manufacturers 24-hour helpline and explain what had happened. I was so worried that they would say that we were to blame and that it would not be covered by the warranty - where would I find the money for another pump? We were both close to tears, and I had just abandoned the girls to look after themselves, though they were now out of the water, (I still had that much sense). Right from the moment I explained what had happened, the person on the other end of the helpline was wonderful, yes, this sort of thing was covered by the warranty; yes, they would ship one out to me immediately; what was the address? It would be with us within 24 hours. We got off the phone thanking her personally, profusely, and praising the company's policy. For the next 24 hours we waited, checking Cole's bloods every two hours all through the day and night, then working out the calculations and adjustments for the amount of insulin his body needed. But no pump arrived. I again called the helpline, who put me on to the Irish branch, and again these new staff were wonderful too. I explained that Cole was now 24 hours off the pump, that we were just a little frazzled as we were manually doing the pump's job and could not put Cole back on to MDI (multiple daily injections) as he reacted badly to basal (background) insulin; we needed the pump asap. They said they would check into it and get back to us. I explained the phone situation, that reception was rubbish, and that I would need to call them, and we arranged a call back in an hour.

"The pump has arrived in Ireland and been sent to the western depot. It should be with you in less than 24 hours."

Again, much thanks. Again, 24 hours of Cole and I being joined at the hip, lacking in sleep and doing all the calculations ourselves while more than a little afraid of getting it wrong or sleeping through the alarm, because even though you think you are so uptight with fear and adrenaline that you will never doze off, you do. Again, no pump. I called the Irish office direct. The man I was dealing with was appalled. I explained that I was fairly sure that I knew now what was happening. Did the courier know that they were shipping life-saving medical equipment? Because I was now sure that the courier was holding the package until they had another delivery to the area. This is a common problem in rural Ireland, couriers do not like to make long journeys for one package. He said he would call them and call me directly back.

"Please do, as I am now beyond sleep-deprived and do not want to go through another night of this. The longer Cole is off the pump and its constant drip feed, the more insulin his body is requiring. We have had to double it in the last 24 hours and I am concerned that my wits might not be as sharp as they should be for all the calculations we are doing."

I did not say that I was scared to death that I would get the calculations wrong, or miss an alarm and cause him to go into a coma, because I did not even want to voice those fears to myself. They were definitely better pushed to the furthest regions of my mind. Before my new friend could call me back, I received another phone call. It was the courier and he was so profusely sorry that he had obviously had the gravity of the situation made very clear to him. He said he would send a driver immediately. I said I would drive to meet him half way as I could not wait. I called back my friend, whose call I had missed while talking to the courier, and told him the latest, and again thanking him and his company.

I drove to meet the courier, who actually turned out to be the shift manager's brother-in-law, and not an employee of the company, but who had been co-opted in as all the vans had already gone out for the day! They had obviously not been going to deliver it that day either, until my new friend had called them and explained, in no uncertain terms, that they were to make the delivery come hell or high water. I called my friend, whose name I can still remember all these years later, and told him that I now had the pump and thanked him again. Then I went home, programmed the pump, connected it to Cole and that night, after about 72 hours since our last proper sleep, both Cole and I fell into an exhausted sleep.

We would not wish this on anyone.

# Chapter 23

It has been absolutely terrifying and heart-breaking, this journey of ours, but we have survived and grown. It is not one that we chose to make. That is, in fact, the point; we made no conscious choices at all in the beginning, we just went with what we were told was safe and effective. We now know that this is not the case. We now know the following:

1. Vaccines do not meet safety standards.
2. That governments admit that vaccines are inherently unsafe.
3. That billions have been paid out to those who have been damaged by vaccines.
4. That the information available on vaccines is produced by the manufacturers, not independent bodies and that this is the information our doctors have.
5. That research has been altered when it showed a causal link between the MMR vaccine and autism.
6. That one of the current vaccines has diabetes mellitus listed as an adverse effect.

What if I had done the research before I gave my children their vaccinations?

Well, we believe that Ariana would never have had Asperger's, and that Cole's chances of ever having diabetes would have been the same as winning the lotto, practically non-existent.

I live in a democratic country, as do many of you reading this, and that means "the practice of social equality". So I have every right to my belief and you to yours. That means that we have the right to be different, and that each of us is equal. No matter what our race, gender, religion, sexual orientation, social status, or our beliefs on health. But what most people are not really aware of, is that this right is constantly under threat. At the moment there is a lot of talk about mandatory vaccination, that those parents who choose not to vaccinate their children should be locked up, and their children taken away from them and forcefully vaccinated. That is not freedom; it is dictatorship and tyranny - one group dictating how another should live their lives and using coercion and fear to achieve their means.

Of course, the question to those who think that vaccines are so wonderful is, "Why do you care if my child does not get them?" If a person believes that vaccines work, then they must believe that their child is protected by the vaccine. It does not matter whether my child gets a disease or not; their child will not get it because they believe that their child is immune, courtesy of the vaccine. They cannot get the disease, end of story. They have no need to be afraid for their child. If they are afraid of their child getting a disease after having been vaccinated, then they must not believe in the efficacy of the vaccine.

However, if vaccines were so wonderful, safe and effective, everyone would be queuing up to have them. There would be no need to create a medical tyranny, where people are forced at gunpoint to vaccinate their children and refused basic liberties, such as education and medical care if they do not. But many of us are not queuing up, not anymore, because many of us have children who have been damaged by "safe" vaccines. Many of us are doing our own research into the safety of vaccines and the dangers of the diseases that they are supposed to prevent; and we are coming to the same conclusions, namely that vaccines are neither safe nor effective, and that the risk of our children being damaged by the disease is far less than the risk of them being damaged by vaccines. Of course, there is a very simple way to test the theory. All it requires is to take two large groups of children - one group vaccinated, whose parents believe in vaccines, and one group unvaccinated, whose parents do not believe in vaccines – and to follow their progress over a long period of time. This would be a scientific method - *"a method of procedure that has characterized natural science since the 17th century, consisting in systematic observation, measurement, and experiment, and the formulation, testing, and modification of hypotheses."* (The New Oxford Dictionary, 1998)

It would also be easy to do as there are already many children worldwide whose parents have made the informed decision not to vaccinate them. It would be ethical too, as these children are never going to have vaccines, their parents have already made this decision, so no choice is been taken away or withheld from them.

It would appear to me that the belief held by the current medical system, which has been around for just over 100 years, that they have categorically found the correct way to health, is a little bit presumptuous. The planet, and medicinal planets and foods, have been evolving for around 4 and a half billion years; humans for over a million years; the current medical beliefs for just 100, and yet they are so sure they are right that they are calling for mandatory vaccination. Of course this cannot be correct, because we are always finding out new things and discovering flaws in our current beliefs: that is what evolving is. We only have to look back at the time when doctors believed bloodletting was the best medical practise, and forced people to submit to it; or when doctors openly promoted the smoking of cigarettes as healthy. We now know that even as the doctors told everyone that smoking was good for you, they were being lied to by the company's manufacturing cigarettes; that these companies already had reports and studies that showed the link between smoking and lung cancer; and that representatives of these companies lied under oath when asked by their governments if there was any connection between smoking cigarettes and lung cancer. So why does everyone have such a hard time believing that the same is not possible now? Human nature has not changed. Some people are still greedy and corrupt, and if they do not have to actually live with the consequences every day, they can happily ignore them for a life with more money and power.

All our pharmaceutical drugs and vaccines have really only been accessible to the masses since the 1940s when penicillin began to be mass produced. That is, less than 80 years. Yet we are being asked to believe, by the medical profession, the pharmaceutical companies and our governments, that they are unquestionably safe and effective. Yet governments worldwide are paying out billions to those damaged by vaccines. David Kessler, a former FDA Commissioner, has estimated that only 6% of all vaccine adverse events are reported. This means that 94% of adverse events are either not recognised as such by the family, because they are told by the medical profession that they are "normal" or unrelated to the vaccine, even though in many cases they are clearly listed as adverse effects on the medical insert which is not given to the parents; or the doctor does not report them because he or she is afraid of the consequences from "up above", and maybe of losing their job or license.

We learn all the time of drugs that have irrevocably damaged or killed people. Remember Thalidomide? It was marketed in the 1960s for morning sickness and interfered with the development and growth of new blood vessels in babies developing in the womb, causing limbs to either not form or to be stumps, deforming eyes and hearts, alimentary and urinary tracts, and causing blindness and deafness. Only 50% of those born with these defects lived. In the late 1990s Vioxx was put on the market, and in less than five years it was withdrawn because it was more than doubling the risk of heart attacks and death. In 2001, Baycol was withdrawn because 50 people had died and 6 million were at risk from the deadly side effects of rhabdomyolysis which causes muscle tissue to dissolve. The list goes on.

Yet many of you may be surprised to know that Thalidomide is still in use. I certainly was. Apparently it is used for treating certain cancers, leprosy, HIV/Aids, Chron's disease, sarcoidosis, graft-versus-host disease, rheumatoid arthritis and a number of skin conditions! And children are still being born with birth defects. So what did the drug companies learn? How did they improve and evolve when faced with the awful side effects of their drug? It would appear that they did not; they just "learnt" how to circumvent the inconvenient problem by marketing the drug under a different name and for a different use. The "side effects" are still the same - children being born with deformities and dying – however, most of them are conveniently in poorer countries now, as that is where the drug is most used, so we do not hear of them.

As we have seen, drug companies have records of fraud and cover-up. We all know governments are plagued by scandals, and vast amounts of doctors are influenced by the drug companies' versions of the facts about the "safety" of their drugs. We are being asked to put our faith and belief in this corrupt and undeniably fraudulent system, to never question anything, nor do our own research. If we do question the safety of vaccines we are labelled "anti-vaxxers", ridiculed and harassed. We are always told that "science" supports vaccines and drugs, yet we are never shown this science; we are expected to just believe it is there because we are told so by those who suppose they are our betters and therefore able to make decisions for us. There are doctors who will not take children into their practise if the parents dare to have an opinion that is different to theirs about vaccines. According to Hippocrates, doctors are supposed to be teachers. They are meant to encourage their patients to look after their own health, to take responsibility for their health and to make healthy choices. Doctors are now taught little to nothing about nutrition - only how to medicate symptoms, not how to teach their patients how to avoid them in the first place and stay healthy. What if we took back into our own hands the responsibility for our own health? What if we started by reading the product insert to the drugs and vaccines we are recommended to take; then we researched diseases, their effects and risks; then considered all our choices and options for health, and made informed decisions about what we felt was the best thing for us to do? What if doctors respected each individual person's right to make an informed decision and supported them in it?

It is funny, too, how any medicinal practise that is outside the current medical model is called "alternative or complimentary", when in fact most of them - acupuncture, traditional Chinese medicine, homeopathy, naturopathy - have been in existence and used for far longer than the current medical model. They have far safer records too. At the moment the third leading cause of death in the world is prescribed pharmaceutical drugs, and since the 1960s, when pharmaceutical drugs and vaccines became widely available, the health of children has steadily worsened with an unprecedented increase in allergies, asthma, autism, auto-immune diseases, and neurological dysfunctions/difficulties in learning such as ADD and ADHD, seizures and many more.

The mainstream media is on the war path at the moment, trying to start a witch hunt against anyone who dares to say that they do not want to give their child a vaccine. They would have you believe that these parents are uneducated idiots while the opposite is in fact true. These parents have done the research, they have spent hours upon hours looking for and researching information on vaccines and they have come to an informed decision that they believe is best for their child and themselves. This is their right, as it is the right of those who wish to vaccinate their children to do so. But one group does not have the right to force their decision on the other. What most people do not know is that the world's mainstream media is more or less now owned by five or six major companies, and those companies have ties and connections with the pharmaceutical industry and the food industry. So it begs the question, "how neutral is the reporting?" In reality it cannot possibly be neutral as funding is coming from these industries. If they withdrew their advertising, for instance, how would the media survive? So they can and do have a say as to what is reported and how.

You only have to look objectively at recent reports on the measles outbreak in Disneyland. Were you told in any of the coverage that, in the last 10 years in the US, only one child and six adults were reported as dying from measles, and of these, only the child was confirmed by an autopsy? Were you told whether this child had contracted wild or vaccine strain measles? No, you were not. You were told to be very afraid of measles, that it is a killer. But in those same 10 years there were 98 deaths reported as due to the measles-vaccine and 694 disabilities reported as due to the measles-vaccine. Did you hear that? (Vaccine Adverse Reporting System (VAERS, 2015). Were you told that anyone getting a vaccine that contains a live virus, such as MMR and whooping cough, can "shed" that virus for many weeks after being vaccinated? And that this "shed" virus can cause people to "catch" measles and whooping cough? No, you were not. Were those who contracted measles at Disneyland tested to see if it was the vaccine strain or wild strain? Again no, or if they were it was not reported. (Loe Fisher, 2014) *(http://www.nvic.org/CMSTemplates/ NVIC/pdf/Live-Virus-Vaccines-and-Vaccine-Shedding.pdf)*

Today I was torn between hope and desperate bone crushing sadness, as Ariana said to me, "I have missed all of my childhood and I will never get it back."

She is right. She has spent most of her childhood living the "what if" game, always trying to work out what people meant and what was expected of her, because she lacked all of the social queues that would have answered these questions. It was exhausting for her, and us, and she has more or less lived on her nerves most of her life. I am desperately sad about this because I can never give it back to her. Yet I also have incredible hope, because for her to be able to "see" this means that she is no longer just living from one agonising moment to the next. It means that she can look back and access what has happened, and look forward and make plans. It means that she has the possibility of being totally independent of us and living her own life, which is something that she, or we, could not have dreamed of before. It means that she is now happy some of the time and can just relax and enjoy the flow of life. If she gets upset by somebody now, she still needs to talk it out with me, but now my role has changed. It is subtle but incredible: more often than not, I do not have to offer up an alternative view point because she has read the situation correctly and made the right decision. She just does not yet have the faith in herself to know that, and because she cannot understand why people are mean and cruel to one another, why they would not look at situations from everyone's perspective and allow them to make the best choice for themselves, she is at a loss to understand some of what goes on in the world. But then, so am I.

"Giving false hope" is often the line that is quoted when medical professionals are talking about alternative health options. They say that it is not right or ethical for alternative health practitioners to treat people with "incurable" health issues, as it gives these people "false hope". I am one of these people because as far as modern medicine is concerned, Asperger's is "incurable". Well, I assure you that living with Asperger's is hell and without "HOPE" we would all be constantly suicidal. I have tried many different health practises to help improve the health and quality of the lives of my children, and I assure you that I have never been offered any "false hope". I have, on the other hand, either been incredibly depressed or frustrated by how the medical profession could not or would not help us. I have had "HOPE" when trying out any option that I had researched and felt may offer help. Never once has it been false, because never once has anything or anyone claimed to be able to heal my children. They have only ever offered to try to help, and offered me much needed support and love as well as hope because some children have improved and are able to function well within society. To me, "HOPE" is everything; it keeps me going; it's what gets me up and out of bed in the morning; it's what keeps me searching to improve my knowledge and myself so that I can help us and others, and make a positive difference in people's lives.

I have always thought that Gandhi was a pretty incredible person, and I think that a lot of you reading this will agree with me. Did you know Gandhi said the following about vaccinations?

*"Vaccination is a barbarous practise and one of the most fatal of all the delusions current in our time. Conscientious objectors to vaccinations should stand alone, if need be, against the whole world, in defence of their conviction."*

Well, I have stepped out of the delusion, because as far as I am concerned, based on my research, that is what it is. I can find no untainted scientific proof that vaccines are safe. In fact, all I have found leads me to believe that they are undeniably unsafe, as is actually admitted on the vaccine inserts and by the governments who pay out compensation to vaccine-injured children.

The following is written in the product insert for GlaxoSmithKline's FLULAVAL vaccine, which is one of the current flu vaccines. (GlaxoSmithKline, 2015)

*Highlights of Prescibing Information. Use in Specific Populations. "Safety and effectiveness of FLULAVAL have not been established in pregnant women or nursing mothers."*

*6.1 "There is the possibility that broad use of FLULAVAL could reveal adverse reactions not observed in clinical trials."*

*6.2 "Postmarketing Experience" "adverse events" "Blood and Lymphatic System Disorders, Eye Disorders, Gastrointestinal Disorders, Chest Pain, Immune System Disorders (eg. anaphylaxis), Infections and Infestations (eg. Cellulitis), Arthritis, Nervous System Disorders (eg. Guillain-Barre syndrome, convulsions/seizures, paralysis, encephalopathy* (swelling of the brain)), *insomnia, respiratory disorders"*

*7.1 "There are insufficient data to assess the concomitant administration of FLULAVAL with other vaccines."*

*8.1 "There are, however, no adequate and well-controlled studies in pregnant women."*

*8.4 "Safety and effectiveness of FLULAVAL in children younger than 3 years of age have not been established".*

*11. Description. "Each 0.5-mL dose from the multi-dose vial
contains 50 mcg thimerosal (<25 mcg mercury)*
*13.1 "FLULAVAL has not been evaluated for carcinogenic or
mutagenic potential."*

*(https://www.gsksource.com/pharma/content/dam/
GlaxoSmithKline/US/en/Prescribing_Information/Flulaval/pdf/*
FLULAVAL.PDF)

So the company admits that there is no "science" to back up
the use of this vaccine in children under 3 years of age, or pregnant
women, or nursing mothers; mercury is still used in it; there is no data
to show that it is safe to be given with other vaccines; and it could
cause cancer or mutations within the body. They did not find out in
their trials, but only later after it was used on the human population,
that it caused a whole list of side effects that are far worse than the
flu. Yet doctors routinely give this vaccine to pregnant women and
young children.

This is just one vaccine insert, as I stated previously, Merck's
insert for its MMR vaccine clearly states that Diabetes Mellitus (type
1 diabetes) is an adverse effect (side effect). So we are been offered
the choice between the risk of getting type 1 diabetes for life instead
of catching measles, mumps or rubella; the risk of having Guillain-
Barré syndrome for life or encephalitis or maybe cancer or goodness
knows what instead of catching the flu. Having done the research
on these and other diseases, and knowing that these diseases can of
course, and sadly do, cause death or disability, and the research on
the "science", or lack of it, behind vaccines and their increasing links
to the rise in current day deaths, disabilities and diseases, I choose to
take my chances with the diseases. This is my choice and my right
to do so. I make no choice for anyone else. I encourage everyone to
research for themselves and make their own informed choice as to
what is best for them and their children.

In this current time, where 1 in 6 children have a learning disability, 1 in 9 has asthma, 1 in 50 has autism, 1 in 400 has diabetes and 1 out of every two men and 1 out of every three women will get cancer, and where auto-immune diseases have tripled in the last 50 years, I would love to see more people looking for the cause to stop the pain and heartache. It cannot all be put down to genetics, as this only accounts for a 3% increase over 10 years. As we have seen, everything is increasing by way more than that. When we are doing our research, we must watch out for "astroturfing". No, this is not a sports pitch covering: it is when political or corporate groups, or someone with a vested interest, disguises themselves as a grass-roots movement (which should be a movement set up by the public with no ties to any industry or governments) and publishes information through blogs, letters to magazines, advertisements, or starts Facebook and Twitter accounts, to fool us, the public, into thinking that there is huge support either for or against an agenda, when there is not. The reason for doing this is to manipulate our opinion; to make us feel that we are wrong because we do not agree with the "majority" opinion. But the "majority" opinion is a paid-for opinion of the vested interest. These "astro-turfers" attack anyone who has a different opinion to theirs, be this doctors, journalists, news organisations, whistle-blowers, politicians or anyone who ask questions.

So, what can we do to make informed decisions and not be manipulated? Well, ask yourself if the article you are reading is using language like "crank", "quacky", "nutty", "paranoid", "conspiracy", "myths", "lies" or "pseudo": these are all favourite terms of astro-turfers. Is the article you are reading talking about the subject matter, or is it just attacking the author? Defamation of character does not show that a theory is incorrect. Is the person or theory you are researching questioning authority? Check whether the information you are looking at is dealing with the subject or is it attacking the person or theory for being anti-authority or anti-government or anti-science, because this is just smoke to stop you looking for independent research or information on the topic you want. The aim is for you to get so frustrated that you stop questioning and just do as you are told. Also, always check whether the group or person that is offering the information you are researching is completely independent or receiving funding from a pharmaceutical company or other vested interest. (Attkisson, 2015) (*https://www.youtube.com/watch?v=-bYAQ-ZZtEU*)

# Chapter 24

So in this present moment, where are we as a family? What is life like? Well, it is always exciting! Though sometimes it is challenging to view it as such. Take, for example, a few weekends ago. I had picked Cole up from school on Friday for the weekend, then driven to meet up with his friend and his Mum so that he could go and stay with them for the weekend. All was fine - the usual "I am alive" texts - and then total radio silence. That is, until 11pm on the Saturday night when Cole called me and in a very subdued voice said, "Mum, I am just changing my set and I do not have a reservoir. I am so sorry. I thought I had checked before I left school. I think I just subconsciously thought, oh weekend, home, lots at home, and forgot that I was not going there first. I am so sorry."

The reservoir is what holds the insulin in the pump, the set is the tubing from the reservoir that ends in a needle inserted into his body so that the insulin can be delivered. The insulin is what keeps him alive.

"Cole, how much insulin is left in the current reservoir?"

"Only 3 units."

Now, Cole's pump alarms him when he has 20 units left. I know this because that is what I have told it to do. His average basal/background insulin consumption is just over 1 unit per hour, so he has plenty of warning: it is also enough to last him through a night should it alarm just after he falls asleep and he sleeps through it. However, not enough, obviously, for a 17-year-old boy who was having much too much fun in the morning when the alarm went off, and so chose to ignore it then, and ignore it again later when he gave insulin for his meals and depleted the reservoir even more. He had done what 17 year olds do: waited till the very last minute to change it. I tried to look on the bright side: at least he had eventually remembered to change it!

"That's less than 3 hours. Empty out your main bag and your bloods bag and see if there are any loose ones lost at the bottom."

"I already have and there aren't."

"Are there any of the filling plungers and needles from old ones that we can use to try and refill this one?" Not advisable at all, but, if possible, it would save us.

"No, I emptied them out before I came when I thought I was checking that I had everything."

Arggh! The one time he chooses not to keep weeks of debris at the bottom of the bag! Usually I run the risk of skewering myself on discarded needles and goodness knows what else when I go to check his bags.

"Ok. I'm on my way. I'll be there in two and half to three hours. Let everyone know what is happening and that you cannot go to sleep."

"I am so sorry. Please do not be angry with me"

"Cole, I am not angry, lovey. I am sorry if I sound like that, it is not that at all. I have just switched into coping, logical mode so that I cannot go into scared mode. Sorry. I love you and I am so glad that you are somewhere safe with people who love you, and not any further away from me or abroad! I'll see you in less than 3 hours and I love you."

"I love you too."

And see, that makes it OK, that my 17 year old son tells me that he loves me.

Then, of course, there was a little discussion between Nicky and I as to who should go and I won because he had hurt his back that morning. As Ariana said, "Dad, your eyes are blood shot, your face has loads of lines on it that normally I do not see, and you are walking like Quasimodo."

He countered with the fact that I had only just been saying before the call how extremely tired I was.

"Well, the adrenaline has kicked in now and I am wide awake again."

So Ariana said that she would come with me to make sure I stayed awake, and off we went at 11.30pm on our 5 hour round trip. See, exciting stuff! Only not exciting like been given thousands of euros; more exciting like succeeding to climb the tree before the bear eats you. We did bring ice cream with us though, chocolate ice cream, because we felt we deserved it.

Then there was the time recently where Ariana could reach neither Nicky nor I when she needed to. Things went a little pear-shaped for her and she just needed to talk things through, but I was at a conference with my phone on silent, and Nicky, who was only just five minutes up the road at work, missed the calls for some reason. I called as soon as I saw the five missed calls. Only half an hour had passed.

"Are you OK?"

"I am now, but I wasn't and I could not get you or Dad. Please do not listen to your voicemail because I was really upset and said some awful things and swore."

Ariana never swears at us, ever.

"I also used one of Cole's needles to scrape my arm."

I went cold and felt the need to move away from everyone and sit down on my own. Before, when she had felt the need to self-harm, I had been able to talk her out of it, but this time I had not been there.

"How bad is your arm?"

"It's OK, just like bramble scratches and I have sprayed it with Hypercal (homeopathic equivalent to disinfectant), so it's clean. I'm OK, Mum. Scratching my arm and having a physical pain on the outside made the pain on the inside easier."

"Do you want me to come home?"

"No, I'm really OK."

Then Nicky arrived home and took over. The thing is, even though Ariana had had a hissy fit, which she had not had in over two years, and even though she had self-harmed, she had come out the other side all by herself and all in under an hour. So, while it was upsetting, it was also amazing! Not so long ago, something like this would have had repercussions for months. Now it was over and done in an afternoon! Again, excitement we could all do without, and wish we never even knew, but so much better than before. And I always know that I am so lucky, because all of my children tell me that they love me, they spend time chatting with me and their friends love visiting too. In fact, when we go away on our summer holidays, we always have masses of the children's friends coming and going, spending hours travelling by plane, train, bus and car just to spend time with us. I am completely honoured and know that I am loved very much. I also know that I must have done something right that teenagers and young adults enjoy my company.

And what of God? Well I no longer hate him but then I no longer believe that he is Him either. Let me explain. When I was little, God was this old man (probably about 49: same age as I am now!), with a long white beard and masses of flowing white hair. Think Gandalf in the Lord of the Rings, but with much more hair and less wrinkles. Well, this God was not a very benevolent fellow; he was a little mercurial really, and his moods were unsettling for me. When I was good, God was happy and I had a lovely time in life, but when life was bad or tough, God was obviously cross with me, because life was only bad for bad people. Bad things only happen to bad people, right? So when all this upheaval was happening in our lives, and life felt like one big manure heap, I was mad as hell with God because my children certainly had not been bad and I was trying my damnedest to live a good life. So why was he being such a vindictive, mean sod and doing this to us? What the hell was he playing at? I hated him.

It took me a lot of soul searching and questioning, and looking at different religions and life in general, to sort out what I believed in and what made me feel right. In the meantime, there was also a lot of ranting and raving around the house and the garden, shaking my fist at the sky and screaming and crying. I really did look like someone demented.

What I have come to believe, for me, is in spirituality minus any particular religion. I have met some very spiritual people in all religions and walks of life, and I have met some zealous fanatics who scared the life out of me. I now believe that there is a universal energy to which we are all connected and from which we all come. I believe that there are many names by which this energy is called: some call it God, some call it Allah, some Buddha. We are all connected, through this energy, to each other and to all life, so I believe that what we call it does not really matter to anyone else but ourselves.

For me spirituality means consciously making the decision every day to lead a loving life - to forgive those who I feel have wronged me, not for them but for me, because I know that if I do not forgive them, I will wither and die and become something I do not want to be; and also to forgive myself, because I am a bit of a perfectionist and so always want to get it "right", which, of course, being just human, I cannot; to aspire to make all my decisions based on a love for all life; the belief that each individual has a right to their beliefs and to choose their path for themselves; to always do my best to help those I can and who want help; to always be open and to examine everything before I make a decision on whether or not it is good for me. Do I always achieve these? Hell no, I am human. But I aspire too.

I have had many mentors along my way who have helped me immensely, some of whom I have not met, such as Mary Morrissey. *(www.marymorrissey.com)* I took one of her online courses, and just loved what she said about the Dali Lama telling her that it was your "special friends" that helped you grow and become a better person, because you had to work at loving them, and that for him the Chinese government was a special friend. Well, I certainly have many special friends, as you can imagine, and they constantly challenge me to grow. She also told of a person who came to her for help, and when she told him that he had to learn to forgive, he was just so cross with this person he could not possibly see how to forgive them. So she said that it really did not matter how he started - a thought or prayer about this person - but he needed to always end it wishing that person well. Well, when she next met him, she could see right off that he was happier, so she asked him what he had done to achieve this. He told her that he had taken her advice and whenever he thought about this "special friend", his thoughts had begun like, "If "special friend" does not get run over by a bus on his way to work, may he have a good day". And I thought, hey, that's brilliant! I can do that. It really does work, because you vent all your anger and hurt in the first part of the sentence, then you put in the aspiring-to-love portion in the last part of the sentence, and over time you find that your anger towards this person diminishes and you can let thoughts of them and your anger/hatred towards them go. You never like or condone what they did, but you can want to want to forgive them so that you can feel better; not for them, for you.

In the beginning, I hated a lot of people for their part in hurting my children, but then I began to realise that hating them was easier than hating myself for being asleep in life and just going through the motions; doing what the collective – society, governments, doctors, the health industry, the pharmaceutical industry, the food industry – told me was best for me and my children, without researching it for myself. I gave away my power, my choice, and my freedom without even being aware of doing so. So I faced myself. I acknowledged that even though I did not have the knowledge I have now, I had inherently questioned giving vaccines to my babies but I still did it because I believed that others knew better than me, were wiser than me. Now I realise that they did not; that we are all equal; that having done the research, I am actually probably more informed than most of those I thought wiser than me; and that I have the right to research and choose how to live my life and what to put into my body and those of my children. Now I try to view them all as my special friends, and I think of another of Ghandi's sayings:

*"It is quite proper to resist and attack a system, but to resist and attack its author is tantamount to resisting and attacking oneself. For we are all tarred with the same brush, and are children of one and the same Creator, and as such the divine powers within us are infinite. To slight a single human being is to slight those divine powers, and thus to harm not only that being but with him the whole world."*

So, every time Asperger's or T1 challenges us and I wish fervently that I had played my hand differently in life, I put my energy into forgiving myself for my part in this, and forgiving all those others -

the doctors, the healthcare industry – for their part. My "resisting and attacking" I aim towards the system - the system that says "vaccines are safe", when they are not, and they know this because they pay out billions in vaccine damages; the system that says "the science" shows that they are safe, without ever producing any independent science; the system that believes all it is told by the pharmaceutical industry, even though they have seen that same industry commit fraud over and over again just to make money at the expense of millions of human lives; the system that bases its public health policy on this fraudulent information; the system that punishes parents who do not follow its vaccination programme for their child by withholding child benefits, even though that same parent will still have to pay their taxes into the scheme; the system that has for years mandated vaccines for children and is now threatening parents to take their children away from them if they do not do as the medical system dictates; the system of governments that have public health programmes that all advocate childhood vaccinations as being "safe" for everyone, yet pay out billions in compensation.

In England recently, GlaxoSmithKline paid out £60 million in vaccine damages to people – 80% children - who were damaged by Pandermix which was one of the vaccines used in Europe for swine flu. (Porter, 2014) *(http://www.ibtimes.co.uk/brain-damaged-uk-victims-swine-flu-vaccine-get-60-million-compensation-1438572)*

It is totally beyond me to explain how governments can tell the public that vaccines are safe when they are paying out vast amounts of money in compensation to people whose lives have been ruined by vaccines; and what you, the reader, need also to know, is that those who are being paid are just the tip of the iceberg. I, and most of the parents I know of who believe that their children have been vaccine damaged, do not have any medical evidence to support any claim, because we were not listened to or believed when we tried to say our child was irrevocably changed for the worse after a vaccine. We cannot go to court because we have nothing but the evidence of our eyes to back us up, because no one in a position of authority would believe us or back us at the time.

I cannot change anyone else in life but I can aim to lead the most loving and best life I can. Hopefully, by doing this it will have a knock on effect on others, and maybe I can, in some small way, help the world to be a better and more loving place.

There is no "greater good", which is often the reason given for trying to make one person do what someone else believes is right, such as vaccinating. I do not believe that I should have to sacrifice my children's health for the greater good of others. There is only that which is good and right for you. You must make the decisions that are right for you and your children. All I am saying is make these decisions consciously, do the research, decide for yourself and do not give away your rights. I wish that I had followed my gut feelings. I wish that I had had access to a resource such as the internet then, so that I could have been able to do the research more easily. I aim never again to follow the herd, to do what I am told is right for the greater good by someone else, nor base my decisions on someone else's beliefs, because we have suffered untold hell (you, my friends, have only heard whispers of it in this story), because I did just that. I fervently hope, that by writing this book and telling our story, I can inspire you, and others, to make informed decisions for your own healthcare. Maybe I can help save you from some of the heartache that we have been through, that would be good.

Our lives are an ongoing challenge, but now it is constantly getting easier with all that we are doing with healthcare options such as homeopathy or nutrition, and we adapt constantly with new information that we learn. Such as the fact that there is an alternative immunisation option called Homeoprophylaxis, utilising homoeopathically prepared substances to stimulate immunity in the body. It has been documented since 1801 when Samuel Hahnemann first used this method. More recently the effectiveness of Homeoprophylaxis has been documented by Dr Isaac Golden in nearly 3,000 children. (Golden, 2004) Also doctors from the Findlay Institute in Cuba carried out a large scale Homeoprophylaxis intervention for Leptospirosis – a disease spread by the urine and faeces of rats and vermin; causing flu-like symptoms which can progress to more serious pathology in the nervous system, kidneys or liver, and can result in death. They administered 2.3 million doses in both 2007 and 2008 and found that the annual incidence, in those treated with homeoprophylaxis, was reduced by 84%. (Bracho, 2010) At the back of this book I have compiled a list of books on this subject for those interested in finding out more.

Today I make informed decisions and I choose what is right for me and my children. I hope that you will also make informed decisions and I wish you all the very best in your lives.

Thank you for taking the time to share our story.

*"Whenever a doctor cannot do good, he must be kept from doing harm."* Hippocrates

# Post Script

I am finding that once I have started to write and impart all this knowledge to you that it is difficult to stop! There are things that I feel we all need to be aware of so as to try and level the playing field when it comes to making informed decisions about our health. So I am just going to impart a few more bits of information here that did not come up in our story for those of you who wish to keep reading.

A "Side effect" or "Adverse effect," does not mean that the effect is rare, which is often what we are told by the medical profession, and what I thought for years. All these statements mean is that they are not the main effect that the manufacturer is marketing the drug for. What I had not thought about is that if a side effect is likely to be increased by 10%, that means 10 people out of 100. If 1000 people take the drug, that means that 100 people are at risk. If 1,000,000 people take the drug, it is 100,000 at risk. Not such a rare thing after all. By the way, <10% means up to 9.9%. It is a really, really good idea to always read the drug insert for all medications you wish to take, including over the counter ones, which I did not do originally. Then if you have an "effect" that is unusual to you, it is possible for you to know if it could be related to the drug you are taking. Often people suffer an "effect" from one drug and when they go to their doctor they are then given another drug for the "effect," and so on, ending up on multiple drugs with little or no benefit.

The information you are given can appear to be magnificent but look carefully at the wording. For instance, if we are told that statins reduce the risk of heart attack by 50%, that is really impressive, no? However, on closer examination of the study we find that there were two groups of 100 people, one group were given statins and the other were not. The groups were followed for three years and during that time two people in the group who did not take statins had heart attacks. In the group who did take the statins one person had a heart attack. So, technically this is a reduction of 50%, but it is far less impressive now that we realise that it is only one person out of 100 over three years. Also, for this reduction of risk of 1 person per 100 over three years, all 100 were at increased risk of the side effects of the statins continuously for three years.

At the current rate of increase in autism some people are predicting that in the next 50 years one in two people will be on the autistic spectrum. This is very worrying as to who will look after these people, many of whom will never be able to join the mainstream work force? Where is the finance going to come from to feed and clothe and house them?

As I have already said, the current accepted medical system is just over 100 years old. However not many people know how it came into existence. It is rather an interesting story. In the late 1800s homeopaths, naturopaths, chiropractors, herbalists, allopaths (medical doctors) and other modalities of healing were all equally available, sought after and used by the public. There were homeopathic hospitals and schools in many countries. Then in the early 1900s a man named Abraham Flexner was commissioned by The Carnegie Institute to travel around America and compile a list of all the medical schools and hospitals and which modality they practised. After Flexner delivered his report The Carnegie Institute donated millions of dollars to those schools and hospitals practising allopathic medicine only. The Rockefeller Foundation followed suit and the allopathic hospitals and schools thrived with massive backing while the others struggled. Over the next few decades the allopathic system was the one that the public "saw" as being the most prestigious as it had the most finance and an assumption was made that it must therefore be the best. As both the Carnegies and Rockefellers were heavily invested in the pharmaceutical industry, this was of enormous benefit to them with the sales of allopathic drugs increasing incredibly.

Cancer is a huge concern to many people in this era, as the WHO predicts that one in two men and one in three women will get cancer. (That, by the way, is also 50% of men and slightly less women. See how words are very important.) Well, what everyone does not know is that the original oral polio vaccine (OPV) was contaminated with a monkey (simian) virus that causes cancer, called SV 40 and this virus has been linked to many cancers in humans. As monkeys are still used in the production of the current inactivated polio vaccine (IPV) it is possible that SV 40 could still be present in some of today's vaccines. The IPV is treated with a 12-day formaldehyde treatment to kill unwanted viruses, however it has been known since the 1960s that SV 40 can survive this.

Nixon declared a war on cancer in the 1970s. In America in 1975 there were 400 new cases of cancer per 100,000 people. In 2007 there were 461 new cases of cancer per 100,000 people. (NIH, 2015) *(http:// report.nih.gov/nihfactsheets/viewfactsheet.aspx?csid=75)* So more people getting cancer today. What we are currently doing is not working.

I am stopping now because if I do not I will never get this information published and out to you so that you can start researching for yourselves.

With love,
Kelly

# Gratitude

There are so many people I feel gratitude towards. If you have been in my life, then I thank you: I have grown because of my experiences.

Of course, I thank Nicky, Théa, Ariana and Cole for sharing this journey with me.

Many thanks to Aoife and Sophie for all their encouragement and help with getting me to write this book and getting it out there.

My parents, Ant and Kate, thank you for your love.

I would not be here but for homeopathy, yoga, nutrition, spirituality and love, so I thank anyone who helped me with these along the way.

To all my new friends at Transformation Books Publishing Services, especially Carrie and Allison for all your encouragement and kindness.

And you, my dear friends, for reading this book. I hope that I have helped you on your journey in life. I wish you love, health and happiness.

# Useful Places to Start Researching

### Homeoprophylaxis

Dr Isaac Golden, Immunisation – Your Child, Your Choice – This is a free online course for parents looking for facts. *http://yescourse.com/store/facts-about-homoeopathic-immunisation/?ref=1030*

*The Solution, Homeopropylaxis: The Vaccine Alternative* by Kate Birch, RSHom(NA), CCH, CMT and Cilla Whatcott, HD (RHom)

*There is a Choice: Homeoprophylaxis* by Cilla Whatcott

*Vaccination & Homoeoprophylaxis? A Review of Risks and Alternatives* by Dr Isaac Golden, PhD

### Films

Bought – *www.boughtmovie.com*

www.fmtv.com is a great site that has a lot of movies concerning health

The Greater Good – *www.greatergoodmovie.org*

Vaccine Nation – www.garynull.com

## Health and Food

*Altered Genes, Twisted Truth* by Steven M. Druker

www.fmtv.com

www.mercola.com

www.naturalnews.com

## Vaccine and Drug Information

*Comparing Natural Immunity with Vaccination* by Trevor Gunn

*Deadly Medicine and Organised Crime* by Peter Gøtzsche

*Dissolving Illusions* by Suzanne Humphries, MD & Roman Bystrianyk

*www.nvic.org*

*The Truth About Vaccines* by Dr Richard Halvorsen

*Vaccines – This book could remove the fear of childhood illness* by Trevor Gunn

*Vaccination Voodoo* by Catherine J Frompovich

## Spirituality

*www.abraham-hicks.com*

www.marymorrissey.com

## *Homeopathy*

www.homeopathy-soh.org (England)

www.homeopathy.org (America)

www.homeopathyoz.org (Australia)

www.homeopathy-ecch.org (Europe)

www.hri-research.org

www.irishhomeopathy.ie (Ireland)


## *Yoga*

www.yogawithadriene.com

# About the Author

I f you are reading this after you have read my book, well, you already know rather a lot about me. However, I thought you might like to know a little bit about what lightens my day and helps to keep me sane.

I love to read and I love to laugh so James Herriot's books are absolutely right up my street and I usually re-read them at least once a year. I also love *The Guernsey Literary and Potato Peel Pie Society* by Mary Ann Shaffer and Annie Barrows. As for music, well my children will tell you, if asked, and even when not asked, that I listen to music from the last century. They are right, but really, has this century produced anything remotely close to Queen and Freddie Mercury's incredible voice range? Or Meat Loaf? Or Bryan Adams? Or Bruce Springsteen? Or Rod Stewart? And then you have the blues legends Ella Fitzgerald, John Lee Hooker, B.B.King, Muddy Waters, Sam Cooke, and Aretha Franklin. I think not.

Then I do a lot of driving and as I love books, audible books come into their own here, especially Ben Aaronovitch's *Rivers of London* series, Benedict Jacka's *Alex Verus* series, Jodi Taylor's *St. Mary's* series, Charlaine Harris' *Sookie Stackhouse* series, Philip Pullman's *Dark Materials,* Garth Nix's *Sabriel* series and of course old favourites such as Richmal Crompton's *Just William* read by Martin Jarvis who also reads P.G. Wodehouse so well. These are all only some of what

I read and listen to amongst researching and providing a free taxi service to my children.

I dislike with a passion, ironing and cleaning and do them under sufferance. I can cook reasonably well but now that the children are older I encourage, and brazenly bribe, them to cook for me as often as I can! To my surprise I have found that I actually quite like writing, I also enjoy learning Spanish, the tenor saxophone and maths, go figure.

I love helping others and so enjoy being a homeopath and am honoured when someone comes to me for help.

But most of all I love spending time with my children, their friends, my husband and my friends and family.

# Endnotes

All websites last accessed November 2015

**Chapter 11**

Scientific Opinion of the Panel on Food Additives, Flavourings, Processing Aids and Food Contact Materials on request from European Commission on Safety of aluminium from dietary intake. The EFSA Journal (2008) 754, 1-34.

Gunn, Trevor. *Vaccines: This Book Could Remove the Fear of Childhood Illness.* SomaWisdom Ltd. 2011. Print.

Frompovich, Catherine J. Vaccination Voodoo: *What YOU Don't Know About Vaccines.* CreateSpace Independent Publishing Platform, 2013. Print.

*The New Oxford Dictionary of English.* Oxford UP, 1998. Print.

Coulter, Harris. "Childhood Vaccinations and Juvenile-Onset (Type-1) Diabetes." Testimony before the Congress of the Unites States, House of Representatives, Committee on Appropriations, subcommittee on Labor, Health and Human Services, Education, and Related Agencies, Washington, D.C. 16 April 1997. Lecture. (*www.whale.to/v/coulter.html*)

## Chapter 14

Dickerson Mayes, Susan, and Angela A. Gorman. "Suicide Ideation and Attempts in Children with Autism." *Research in Autism Spectrum Disorders* 7.1 (2013): 109-119. Print.


## Chapter 15

Halvorsen, Richard. *The Truth About Vaccines, making the right decision for your child.* Gibson Square Books Ltd, 2009 second edition of 2007. Print.

Humphries, Suzanne, and Bystrianyk, Roman. *Dissolving Illusions: Disease, Vaccines, and The Forgotten History.* CreateSpace Independent Publishing Platform, 2013. Print.

Gunn, Trevor. *Vaccines: This Book Could Remove the Fear of Childhood Illness.* SomaWisdom Ltd. 2011. Print.

*http://www.cdc.gov/polio/about/index.htm last accessed 02/12/15*

*http://www.who.int/mediacentre/factsheets/fs114/en/*


## Chapter 16

*The New Oxford Dictionary of English.* Oxford UP, 1998. Print.

Hooker B: **Measles-mumps-rubella vaccination timing and autism among young african american boys: a reanalysis of CDC data.**

*Transl Neurodegener* 2014, **3**:16.

*http://www.naturalnews.com/046566_autism_MMR_vaccine_CDC_whistleblower.html#ixzz3BFC7Low9.*

*http://www.morganverkamp.com/august-27-2014-press-release-statement-of-william-w-thompson-ph-d-regarding-the-2004-article-examining-the-possibility-of-a-relationship-between-mmr-vaccine-and-autism/*

Morgan Verkamp LLC. *Statement of William W. Thompson, Ph.D., Regarding the 2004 Article Examining the Possibility of a Relationship Between MMR Vaccine and Autism*. Ohio: Morgan Verkamp, 27 August 2014.

*http://www.cdc.gov/*

*https://www.youtube.com/watch?v=uNWTOmEi_6A*

*http://www.cdc.gov/ncbddd/AboutUs/biographies/Boyle.html*

*http://www.cdc.gov/employment/pdf/Job_Profile_Pediatricians.pdf*

*http://www.mercknewsroom.com/news-release/corporate-news/merck-announces-appointment-dr-julie-gerberding-executive-vice-president*

*http://www.thecoli.com/threads/parents-cdc-whistleblower-says-mmr-shot-raises-autism-risk-in-african-american-babies-3-n-under.243392/*

Stephen A. Krahling and Joan A. Wlochowski v. Merk. U.S. District Court for the Eastern District of Pennsylvania. 27 Aug. 2010. Print.

*http://www.naturalnews.com/048402_measles_vaccine_scientific_fraud_court_documents.html*

*http://www.supremecourt.gov/opinions/10pdf/09-152.pdf*

*http://www.nvic.org/injury-compensation.aspx*


*http://www.who.int/bulletin/volumes/89/5/10-081901/en/*

*http://nsnbc.me/wp-content/uploads/2013/05/BSEM-2011.pdf*


Hedrich, A. W. "MONTHLY ESTIMATES OF THE CHILD POPULATION "SUSCEPTIBLE'TO MEASLES, 1900–1931, BALTIMORE, MD." *American Journal of Epidemiology* 17.3 (1933): 613-636.

Difficulties in Eliminating Measles and Controlling Rubella and Mumps; A Cross-Sectional Study of a First Measles and Rubella Vaccination and a Second Measles, Mumps, and Rubella Vaccination. *(www.ncbi.nlm.nih.gov/pmc/articles/PMC3930734/)*

241

*Global Manual on Surveillance of Adverse Events Following Immunizations.* World Health Organization, 2014. Print.

Gunn, Trevor. *Comparing Natural Immunity with Vaccination.* Informed Parent Publications, 2006. Print.

Gunn, Trevor. *Vaccines: This Book Could Remove the Fear of Childhood Illness.* SomaWisdom Ltd. 2011. Print.

"MMR II (MEASLES, MUMPS, and RUBELLA VIRUS VACCINE LIVE)." Merck Sharp & Dohme Corp., a Subsidiary of Merck & Co., Inc., 1 June 2014. Web. *<https://www.merck.com/product/usa/pi_circulars/m/mmr_ii/mmr_ii_pi.pdf>*

## Chapter 18

Smits, Tinus. *Autism, Beyond Despair: Homeopathy has the Answers.* Emryss Publishers, 2010.

Vermeulen, Frans. *Monera: Kingdom Bacteria and Viruses.* Emryss Publishers, 2005.

Ter Meulen, V. "Measles virus and Crohn's disease: view of a medical virologist." *Gut* 43.6 (1998): 733-734.

Gunn, Trevor. *Vaccines: This Book Could Remove the Fear of Childhood Illness.* SomaWisdom Ltd. 2011. Print.

*www.thinktwice.com*

## Chapter 19

*www.medicalkidnap.com*

*www.thetruthaboutcancer.com*

## Chapter 22

Gøtzsche, Peter C. *Deadly Medicines and Organised Crime: How Big Pharma Has Corrupted Healthcare.* CRC Press, August 28, 2013.

Horton, Richard. "The Dawn of McScience." *The New York Review of Books* March 11, 2004 (2004). Web. *<http://www.nybooks.com/articles/archives/2004/mar/11/the-dawn-of-mcscience/>.*

Angell, Marcia. "Drug Companies & Doctors: A Story of Corruption." *The New York Review of Books* January 15, 2009 (2009). Web. *<http://www.nybooks.com/articles/archives/2009/jan/15/drug-companies-doctorsa-story-of-corruption/>.*

Kassirer, Jerome P. *On the Take: How Medicine's Complicity with Big Business Can Endanger Your Health.* Oxford UP, 2005. Print.

"Diphtheria - The Disease." *Immunization, Vaccines and Biologicals.* World Health Organization. Web. *<http://www.who.int/immunization/topics/diphtheria/en/index1.html>.*

*http://www.who.int/immunization/monitoring_surveillance/burden/vpd/surveillance_type/passive/pertussis/en/*

*http://www.whale.to/vaccines/cot_death.html*

Scheibner, Viera. *Vaccination 100 Years of Orthodox Research.* First Australian Edition ed. Co-Creative Designs, 1993. Print.

"MEASLES, MUMPS, and RUBELLA VIRUS VACCINE LIVE." *MMR II.* Merck Sharp & Dohme Corp., a Subsidiary of Merck & Co., Inc., 1 June 2014. Web. *<http://www.merck.com/product/usa/pi_circulars/m/mmr_ii/mmr_ii_pi.pdf>*

## Chapter 23

*The New Oxford Dictionary of English.* Oxford UP, 1998. Print.

*https://vaers.hhs.gov/index*

Loe Fisher, Barbara. "The Emerging Risks of Live Virus & Virus Vectored Vaccines: Vaccine Strain Virus Infection, Shedding & Transmission." *National Vaccine Information Center.* 2014. Web. *<http://www.nvic.org/ CMSTemplates/NVIC/pdf/Live-Virus-Vaccines-and-Vaccine-Shedding.pdf>.*

"FLUVAL (Influenza Vaccine)." *GSK Source.* GlaxoSmithKline, 1 June 2015. Web. 1 Nov 2015.

*https://www.gsksource.com/pharma/content/dam/GlaxoSmithKline/US/en/ Prescribing_Information/Flulaval/pdf/FLULAVAL.PDF*

Attiksson, Sharyl. "Astroturf and manipulation of media messages." Online video clip. *YouTube.* YouTube, 6 Feb. 2015.

*https://www.youtube.com/watch?v=-bYAQ-ZZtEU*

## Chapter 24

*www.marymorrissey.com*

Porter, Tom. "Brain-Damaged UK Victims of Swine Flu Vaccine to Get £60 Million Compensation." *International Business Times.* 2 Mar. 2014. Web. *<http://www.ibtimes.co.uk/brain-damaged-uk-victims-swine-flu-vaccine-get-60-million-compensation-1438572>.*

Golden, Isaac. *Homoeoprophylaxis: A Fifteen Year Clinical Study.* AURUM, 2004.

Bracho, Gustavo, et al. "Large-scale application of highly-diluted bacteria for Leptospirosis epidemic control." *Homeopathy* 99.3 (2010): 156-166.

## Post Script

"NIH Fact Sheets Home-Cancer." *NIH Research Portfolio Online Reporting Tools.* 29 Mar. 2013. Web. 11 Nov. 2015. *http://report.nih.gov/ nihfactsheets/viewfactsheet.aspx?csid=75*

Made in the USA
Columbia, SC
20 November 2017